Religious education 7–11

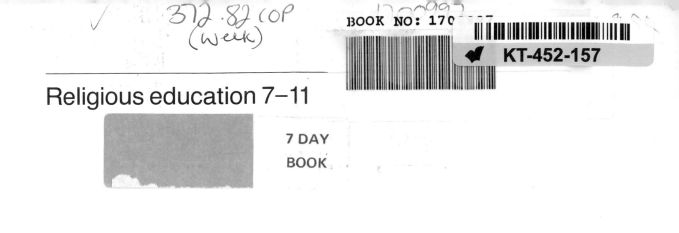

The place of religious education in the primary curriculum is an ambiguous one for many teachers. Terence Copley, well known for his many publications in the RE field, here clarifies the legal framework, including problem areas like the withdrawal of children from the subject. He looks at the key principles and concepts involved in teaching the main areas of religious education – world faiths, Christianity, education for spiritual development and so on – and also at practical issues of classroom organisation, for instance how to obtain artefacts and how to prepare for visits to places of worship. The book contains work on teacher competencies to enable teachers to monitor their own performance and hints on how RE work can fulfil curriculum requirements in other subjects.

Terence Copley is currently senior lecturer in RE at the School of Education, Exeter University.

Curriculum in primary practice series
General editor: Clive Carré

The Curriculum in primary practice series is aimed at students and qualified teachers looking to improve their practice within the context of the National Curriculum. The large format, easy to use texts are interactive, encouraging teachers to engage in professional development as they read. Each contains:

- Summaries of essential research
- Transcripts of classroom interactions for analysis and discussion
- Activities for individual and group use

While all primary teachers will find these books useful, they are designed with the needs of teachers of the 7 to 11 age group particularly in mind.

Other titles include:

Science 7–11
Clive Carré and Carrie Ovens

Music 7–11
Sarah Hennessy

Forthcoming titles in 1995:

English 7–11
David Wray

Religious education 7–11

Developing primary teaching skills

Terence Copley

London and New York

First published 1994
by Routledge
11 New Fetter Lane, London EC4P 4EE

Simultaneously published in the USA and Canada
by Routledge
29 West 35th Street, New York, NY 10001

Typeset in Palatino by Solidus (Bristol) Limited
Printed and bound in Great Britain by
Clays Ltd, St Ives PLC

British Library Cataloguing in Publication Data
A catalogue record for this book is available from the British Library

Library of Congress Cataloging in Publication Data
A catalogue record for this book has been requested

ISBN 0-415-10125-5

Contents

Preface

Surely RE is covered by the PSE programme?

If RE's everywhere in the curriculum I suppose I can do anything I like and call it RE.

I'm rather confused about my own beliefs, so I leave RE to the teachers who're sure.

As a non-Christian I couldn't in conscience teach RE.

We may all have heard these sorts of remarks in primary school staffrooms by teachers who for various reasons are diffident about treating RE as they treat other subjects. At its extreme I saw this attitude in an INSET session I was leading. During a perfectly routine and uncontroversial discussion I noticed a middle-aged infants teacher in the group *crying*. The reason was not because she had been sent on the course by her head – though this was true! – but because she had never faced up to all sorts of doubts and confusions in her own mind about RE and her own religious beliefs and disbeliefs, nor had she studied RE since her own childhood, and all these issues had suddenly come to the surface. She was positively and helpfully supported at the time by colleagues on the course, but I have often wondered what happened to her afterwards. This book is for her, and all teachers with similar doubts and confusions. It aims to set the record straight for RE, which would probably not, as many claim, get the prize for the hardest subject to teach, but could well be the winner of the award for the most misunderstood or the one for which teachers are least prepared during their initial training.

It is sometimes said that children are antipathetic or apathetic towards religion and therefore to RE. This is misleading. What children are hostile to or at best politely indifferent towards is having religion thrust down their throats. Experience teaches the teacher that children find fascinating the questions religions grapple with, the stories that religions tell, and the opportunity to question and discuss or argue with religious people or to visit religious shrines and sites. Much that religions have to tell in a secular society is 'new' to children and far from being hostile to RE they are readily prepared to be interested in the issues raised.

Some teachers find that their own attitudes towards RE stem from their personal attitudes – of enthusiasm, dislike and all the stages in between – towards religion itself. Many are very much aware that they received insufficient initial training in RE and all teachers are subject to the pressures imposed by the delivery of the National Curriculum. There is sometimes an understandable tendency to reduce RE to a very low priority in the classroom.

This book is intended to provide theoretical and practical help to enable more effective teaching and learning in classroom RE. It may also be useful to students in training and to staff groups undertaking school-based INSET.

Religions have learned over many millennia long before popular education or national curricula existed to use story, to use symbols, to use simple teaching, to put over profound truth claims. Without that they would have been intellectual hobbies for a minority and not world religions at all. Religious education can cash in on these teaching insights from religions as well as using the latest, modern educational techniques and technologies of delivery and assessment. In the primary school, RE is likely to continue to be taught in wider topics as well as in the discrete subject units with older children currently favoured by government. I have tried to write with both user contexts in view, because they do not constitute an either–or approach to the subject but complement each other. Whatever the current government trend in teaching and learning might be, there are good educational reasons for creating some RE-led topics. Without them the rather random appearances of RE within other topic work (journeys, our village, India, etc.) are not likely in themselves to provide sufficient or coherent understanding of religious material nor to meet the require-ments of agreed syllabuses or of OFSTED inspection. When RE appears as a topic leader or as a legitimate part of another project, sensitively undertaken, teachers and pupils will enjoy learning together and parents will be equally intrigued by the issues and questions that are raised at home in the course of the exploration.

Terence Copley
School of Education,
University of Exeter, 1994

Acknowledgements

The activity 'River creature' in Unit 6 was devised by Michael Beesley who has given permission for it to appear here.

Quotations have been made from various agreed syllabuses for RE:

- The KS2 map from the Newcastle upon Tyne syllabus available from Newcastle upon Tyne LEA, Civic Centre, Barras Bridge, Newcastle upon Tyne NE1 9PU
- The KS1 EKSS from the Sefton syllabus, available from Sefton LEA, Education Offices, Burlington House, Crosby Road North, Waterloo, Liverpool L22 0LG
- The KS1 EKSS from Newham syllabus, available from Newham LEA, Education Offices, 379 High Street, Stratford, London E15 4RD
- The KS1 and 2 maps from Solihull syllabus, available from Solihull LEA, Education Offices, PO Box 20, Council House, Solihull B91 3QU

Various assessment tasks have been included from the FARE (Forms of Assessment in Religious Education) Report by permission of the FARE Project, University of Exeter School of Education, Exeter EX1 2LU.

The activity 'Loving lollipops' by Kathy Raban is a shortened version of one that appears in John Hammond *et al. New Methods in RE Teaching: An Experiential Approach*, 1990, Oliver & Boyd, Edinburgh.

The Index was prepared by Gill Copley

By no means least I should like to acknowledge the constructive support and comments at the various drafting stages of this book by the series editor, Clive Carré, and the many real but anonymous children with whom I have over the years shared that mutual curiosity and excitement about what makes human beings tick that must be the backbone of any effective RE.

Unit 1

The legal framework for RE

Until the 1988 Education Reform Act the joke used to be that RE was the only subject that had to be taught – hence the only compulsory subject – but at the same time the only one that parents could opt their children out of and teachers could opt out of teaching – hence also legally the only optional subject. How much do you know about the 1988 Act and the position of RE now? Check your answers with those in Appendix III, p. 90.

THE 1988 ACT: quiz

1 changed the legal name of the classroom subject from religious instruction to religious education.   Yes ☐ No ☐

2 did not remove the right of parents to withdraw their children from RE.   Yes ☐ No ☐

3 continued the local arrangements for RE, with a locally agreed syllabus at LEA level rather than a national syllabus.   Yes ☐ No ☐

4 introduced national attainment targets for RE.   Yes ☐ No ☐

5 banned teaching about denominational differences.   Yes ☐ No ☐

6 made the creation of Standing Advisory Councils on RE (SACREs as they are known, pronounced sacré, rather like a French swear word) at LEA level, including teacher representation, mandatory.   Yes ☐ No ☐

7   did not permit a serving teacher to serve on any panel of a SACRE except the Teacher's Panel.   Yes ☐ No ☐

8   continued the 1944 requirement that RE must be provided for all pupils in all county and voluntary schools.   Yes ☐ No ☐

9   would permit the use of a diocesan or other syllabus subject to governors' agreement in a voluntary aided or special agreement school.   Yes ☐ No ☐

10   prescribes how RE is to be organized and taught in school.   Yes ☐ No ☐

The essence of the 1988 Act was to preserve RE as an entitlement for all pupils and to accord it status as a 'basic subject' alongside the National Curriculum. The intention was to ensure 'that RE has equal standing in relation to the core and other subjects within a school's curriculum'. This was again affirmed in the Dearing Report (1993). One may wonder whether its delivery in many schools has been faithful to this intention.

SACREs

The duty of the Standing Advisory Council on RE is, as its name implies, to advise the local authority on RE and collective worship, on issues relating to these raised by the LEA or the SACRE. DFE Circular 3/89 goes on to explain that the sorts of issues these might include are: reviewing provision for RE in the schools of the LEA, methods of teaching RE, choice of teaching materials and provision of teacher training, including INSET, in RE. For further details of how SACREs work, see Appendix IV on p. 93. SACREs can be useful allies. If involved by the LEA, they can support a school if it has to deal with an unreasonable parental complaint. Some SACREs have carried out surveys of provision for RE in schools in their LEA – these have helped the worst resourced schools to lobby for and acquire better provision. Some SACREs have lobbied the LEA or government to make points about the legal position of RE or the provision of advisory support. In one case at least the appointment of a county RE Adviser after a vacancy caused by promotion of the previous holder was only achieved by persistent SACRE lobbying in the face of a proposed LEA cut of the job.

ACTIVITY 1.1

Obtain a copy of the latest annual SACRE report for your LEA (SACREs include representation from grant maintained schools if your school is in this category). Is any member of SACRE known to any of your staff? What single issue in the report do you think was the most important of their activities for the year in question?

Are there issues that the SACRE could address that might help RE in your school?

If so, why not make contact with one of the teacher representatives, or someone on another panel you might know?

AGREED SYLLABUSES

This quaint name for the RE syllabus stems from the past, whereby the various churches and the LEA tried to agree a syllabus for undenominational teaching of RI or Religious Instruction, as it then was, in schools. Not surprisingly in the early years of the twentieth century when church–chapel, i.e. Anglican–Free Church, rivalries were still strong they could often only agree on the Bible! This accounts in part for the dominance of the Bible in RE teaching into the 1950s and 60s. Polls at the time showed that even parents who had no church links at all wanted their children to be taught the Bible. Nowadays agreed syllabuses are drawn up by bodies comprising four panels with the same constituencies as those of the SACRE, with strong professional representation and members from various faiths in addition to Christianity and often from a secular humanist stance as well. Not surprisingly, agreed syllabuses have broadened considerably in their content and recommended teaching methods. Often the actual prescriptive syllabus is very brief, but there may be a larger section or handbook of ideas, suggested resources, useful addresses, etc., for its implementation. The 1988 Act required that all syllabuses adopted from 29 September 1989 must 'reflect the fact that the religious traditions in Great Britain are in the main Christian whilst taking account of the teaching and practices of the other principal religions represented in Great Britain'. In a sense, this is the first Act to require teaching of world faiths and so even an LEA like Devon, which might to some outsiders bring to mind a white, Christian, rural stereotype, produced a syllabus in 1992 in line with these ERA provisions. In the Devon document a section on promoting quality in RE is followed by an educational framework, then sections on planning RE at each key stage, then on reviewing RE and then a section setting out key concepts and areas of knowledge in six major world religions.

It must be emphasized that whatever its contents, an agreed syllabus is a legal document with a status of its own. One major criterion for OFSTED inspection of RE in a school is its conformity to the agreed syllabus. During 1994 SCAA produced model syllabuses for RE, not as statutory documents but as advice to LEAs drawing up a new local syllabus.

ACTIVITY 1.2

Obtain a copy of the agreed syllabus applicable to your school. When was it last revised?

Did you already know its requirements for the key stage you work in?

STAGE 1 – (5–7)

CONCEPTS	**Beliefs:** To introduce an understanding of God with special reference to Christianity. **Importance of Religion:** To recognise the importance of religion to believers. **Morality:** To recognise and understand the difference between right and wrong. **Forgiveness:** To appreciate the need to give and receive forgiveness.
KNOWLEDGE **To study or to know about:**	**Sacred Writings:** Selected Old Testament and New Testament stories. **Prayer:** The meaning and formulation of prayer and ways in which people pray including the Lord's Prayer. **Worship:** The ways in which people worship in the local community. **Celebration and Festivals:** Religious festivals and celebrations. **Ceremonies:** Family ceremonies. **Symbols:** Some religious symbols, for example the Cross.
SKILLS	**Language:** To recognise that religion has a language of its own. **Sources:** To use a variety of sources providing information about religion. **Self-expression:** To begin to express in a variety of ways, feelings, opinions and beliefs. **Empathy:** To enter imaginatively into the experiences of others. **Reflection:** To think about one's experiences.
ATTITUDES	**Respect and Self-respect:** To value oneself as an unique human being and to give due worth to other people. **Integrity:** To value truth and be honest about one's feelings, attitudes and actions. **Enquiry:** To develop an enquiring approach to life generally and in particular to the fundamental and religious questions life poses. **Social Awareness:** To develop an appreciation of the service, care and concern of others. **Social Responsibilities:** To develop an awareness of one's own capacity to contribute to the well-being of others in the family, school and community. **Forgiveness:** To appreciate the need to give and receive forgiveness. **Tolerance:** To develop a respect for people and their right to believe. **Ecological Responsibility:** To develop a respect for the natural world as God's creation. **Ecological Responsibility:** To develop a respect for the natural world as a place shared with fellow human beings.

HUMAN EXPERIENCE	**Spiritual Experiences:** To respond to spiritual experiences and to examine questions derived from human experience. **Self-awareness and Responsbility to Others:** To seek to give practical expressions to experiences of self-awareness and responsibility to others and building relationships in the wider world. **Emotions:** To appreciate the range of human emotions as experienced by the children.

Figure 1.1 Key Stage 1 map, Solihull syllabus

PARENTAL COMPLAINTS AND WITHDRAWALS

The basic complaints machinery for RE is no different from other subject areas. A parent should contact the headteacher for redress and failing that can appeal to the LEA in the case of a LEA maintained school. The LEA will then investigate, usually via its RE Adviser, involving the SACRE or not according to local practice. Appeal lies beyond to the Secretary of State, a long way from the school where the complaint began. But although a tiny minority of parents seem able to demonstrate a capacity to be unreasonable in a variety of situations, schools that are working to the agreed syllabus are safe. Where complaints arise, the sort of allegations that are made include:

• no RE is being done, clearly potentially a valid complaint.
• a parent objects to a faith being taught about – in one such recent complaint the objection was that Islam was being taught and although the agreed syllabus required this, the matter still received local press coverage.
• fundamentalist religious parents object to some activity connected with the 'Satanic' e.g. a ghost story or celebration for Hallowe'en.
• it is alleged that insufficient time is being allocated to the teaching of Christianity.
• more rarely, it is alleged that too much time is being allocated to the teaching of Christianity.

Parental concerns about RE are discussed more fully in Unit 9, p. 79.

 ACTIVITY 1.3

Dear Teacher,
   I am writing to express my concern about my daughter's RE this year. As far as I can tell she did no RE at all in Term 1, except for making Christmas decorations and practising carols. Then in Term 2 she did quite a lot about Divali as part of a

project on India. This term, so far, she has done nothing, except that I gather the headteacher used the story of David and Goliath in an assembly about bullying.

If what she has told me is correct I have to say that I do not consider that she has received adequate RE, within the spirit or the letter of the 1988 Act. Such RE as she has received has lacked coherence and it has failed to deal with Christianity as required by law.

I look forward to your comments on this.

Yours sincerely,

A.N.R. Ticulate
(Parent)

How can schools protect themselves against this sort of complaint? Could this sort of complaint be made about RE in any part of your school? To what extent is the designation of one teacher as RE co-ordinator in the school a protection against this sort of complaint? Write a rough draft to help your headteacher to answer this letter.

In practice formal complaints about RE are rare but they can be time consuming, even where they are unjustified.

WITHDRAWN CHILDREN!

As we have seen, the parent has the right to withdraw a child from RE. This includes the right for the child to receive 'RE' elsewhere off the premises at the beginning or end of the school day. It is likely that retaining this right reflects confusion in the Act itself. In the old days there was RI, Religious Instruction, from which it could be argued children might have needed protection. In contrast RE, Religious Education, carries with it all the open-ended opportunities and entitlement we associate with education, not least the development of tolerance and respect for others whose views and life-style differ from our own. Legally allowing children to be withdrawn from RE as opposed to the old RI suggests that the two were being confused by the legislators. Schools that encourage parents not to withdraw their children from RE are properly emphasizing education not indoctrination – but in the end the parent can still opt the child out. This is commonly, but not universally, done by Jehovah's Witness parents (for details about their beliefs, see Unit 9 and Appendix III), and occasionally by parents from other sects, or by a minority of atheist parents. It is a pity that a parent can block their child's entitlement to know about the place of religion and religions on the global and UK scene and the historic Christian basis of our culture, but the right to avoid RE is currently the law. It makes it all the more important that all parents should know and understand what we are and are not trying to do in RE.

One reason, perhaps sufficient in itself, for RE to be seen as an entitlement for all children is that without the working knowledge of major religions which RE can provide over the 11 years of compulsory schooling, it becomes barely possible to understand even the daily newspapers or TV news, when one sees the potent influence of religion, sometimes for good, sometimes for ill, in different parts of the planet.

Religion in the headlines in the recent past

CARDINAL SPEAKS OUT ON ABORTION
CULT SHOOT OUT IN TEXAS
WILL SHI'ITES RECOGNISE ISRAEL?
SIKH BACKLASH FEARED IN PUNJAB
LATEST DEAD SEA SCROLLS
SEARCH FOR ARK CONTINUES
CHURCH OF SCOTLAND GENERAL ASSEMBLY RECEIVES PM

What, however, if pupils raise a religious question spontaneously in some other area of work? Does the teacher have to shoo the 'withdrawn children' out of the room before plunging into discussion? Fortunately DFE Circular 3/89 is quite clear that such enquiries and the follow-up are unlikely to constitute RE as defined by law. It advises headteachers to liaise with withdrawing parents about the issues to which the parent objects to the child being taught directly or indirectly and the practical implications of withdrawal. Class teachers and heads are under no legal obligation to provide an alternative learning experience for withdrawn children, so the book corner or the library might be a quite suitable place for them to be occupied in RE time.

ATTITUDES OF TEACHERS AND PUPILS TO RE

As in all areas of knowledge, nobody is neutral in religion – neither teacher, nor pupil, nor parent. Each of us will approach religion as a believer, or as a sceptic, or as a 'don't know', but never as a neutral, entirely objective bystander. Sometimes student teachers, and more experienced teachers too, worry about whether they ought in conscience to exercise their right to withdraw from teaching RE because they are not sure what they believe, or they might be quite certain that they are sceptical about religion. This is a professional misunderstanding that, like the withdrawal clause in the Act, goes back to the old religious instruction days. Conscience would of course require anyone to withdraw from preaching or transmitting *as true* a faith they did not hold. But education, including religious education, is not about transmitting ultimate truths but about helping children to make sense of the world in which they live. RE is concerned to look at human experience in the past and present and encourage the question 'Is it true?' rather than short-circuit the whole process by giving children answers before they can even see the importance of the questions. In this sense RE shares common ground with science, for many scientists would indicate that their science has no universally agreed ultimate truths. Even in history the Battle of Hastings could one day be re-dated! RE is concerned with helping children to see religion as a potent world force, as a living UK force, and as one option for personal living. 'Is this true?', or 'Is this bit of it true?' are the questions that make the exercise so interesting!

In this sense the committed Christian, the agnostic, the Muslim, the atheist, the Sikh are all potentially capable of teaching RE and all have something to contribute. We do not balk at teaching about life in a medieval monastery in history because we have not been nuns or monks, nor about teaching French because we are not French, nor about doing a topic on India even though we may not have been there in person. We may not be religious 'in person' but as we attempt to explore with children some of the diverse questions and possible answers that religions present about the human situation, we are not performing a religious function but an educational one. We are offering choice and developing awareness and sensitivity to the views of others. These are value judgements about what is worth while and there are others that we may need to discard or adopt. Inappropriate in the opinion of many teachers would be the views:

that it is better to be religious than not;

and

that one religion is better than all the others.

Teachers may personally hold either or both of these views, but they are personal religious value judgements and not professional educational ones. Educational value judgements worth considering as a basis for RE might include:

that religions represent such a richness of human experience that like art, music and literature, they are worth studying as part of our heritage;

that every child is entitled to know about their option on a religious way of life;

that it is better to be conscious of one's beliefs and values, whether religious or secular, than to act and decide on the basis of values of which one is only dimly aware;

and

that irrespective of our own personal religious or non-religious attitude to life, we need an awareness of the position of Christianity in shaping our culture in order to interpret our laws, music, literature, architecture and art properly. To avoid this would be analogous to refusing to look around a cathedral or listen to a requiem mass or look at a painting of the Last Supper simply because one happened to be an atheist.

Of course, these value judgements for RE are not written on tablets of stone! It may be argued, for instance, that intuition has its own proper place in spiritual awareness and should be encouraged. Being dimly aware of something we believe in or aspire to may in some instances be the only position humans can in honesty hold to; in other circumstances it may be an excuse for shoddy thinking. What matters is that we as teachers bring into the open our value judgements about RE and consider how far they are educationally defensible.

 ACTIVITY 1.4

Discuss with a small group of primary children what they think RE is about. Is there a common pattern to their response? Where do you think they have got their views from? Does it relate to their school work in the last year? If you know their teachers, find out whether their teachers hold the same view of what RE is about.

How far do you think it professionally appropriate or necessary for teachers to declare their beliefs or lack of them to the class? Is there a parallel to expressing political views here or not?

If you teach in a school, you might consider whether it is the religious teachers who spend the most time doing RE with their classes. That might reflect their enthusiasm, but might it also reflect the misconceptions of the non-religious teachers that somehow this is an area they can't join in? If possible discuss with a group of teachers what their attitudes to RE are and how they have evolved.

ATTAINMENT TARGET FRAMEWORK

Whilst not prescribing national attainment targets for RE, the 1988 Act and follow-up did not disallow local (and equally binding) targets. The SCAA model attainment targets for RE are:

1   learning about religion
2   learning from religion.

In the aftermath of the Act, various LEAs and RE bodies were worried that by not having ATs, programmes of study, etc., RE might be marginalized in the minds particularly of busy primary teachers and therefore neglected in the classroom under the many new post-Act pressures. It was also felt that a focus on ATs and assessment processes could actually enhance the teaching and learning process. Various different schemes arose, including one at the Regional RE Resources Centre, based at Westhill College, Birmingham, and one at Exeter University. Each scheme had a number of 'client' LEAs, but was used and modified by others. Other LEAs worked independently to produce their own schemes. So while there is no uniformity in assessment in RE, there is significant work that can help teachers in the delivery of the subject. Assessment in RE is considered in more detail in Unit 8.

ACTIVITY 1.5

Dorset Agreed Syllabus (1992) entitled *REaction, REflection, REsponse* identified two ATs and associated programmes of study and statements of attainment in RE:

AT1   Understanding and evaluating values, commitments and questions of meaning

AT2   Knowledge, understanding and evaluation of religious belief, practice and expression.

The document goes on to describe an RE contribution to English (ATs 1 to 3), Art, Music, History, Geography, Technology and Science and to cross-curricular themes: Citizenship, Health Education, Environmental Education, Careers Education and Economic and Industrial Understanding (pp. 56 to 60).

If you are working in a school, consider how your RE work this term might contribute to one or more of these areas. Unit 2 develops more thoroughly the relationship of RE to the National Curriculum.

Planning for RE

AT SCHOOL LEVEL

Four crucial documents should affect planning for RE. These are the NCC documents, *Starting Out With the National Curriculum,* and *Religious Education: A local curriculum framework,* the local agreed syllabus for RE and the school's own policy statement on RE.

Starting Out With the National Curriculum provides the overall curriculum context within which RE operates – and deals specifically with RE on pages 6, 25 and 56f. A brief summary of the legal position is followed by a statement of general aims for RE: that pupils 'should understand the teachings and practices of Christianity and the other world religions' and 'be encouraged to develop their own beliefs and values'. While pointing out that syllabuses are devised and agreed locally it identifies various *key concepts* which have arisen in most syllabuses:

beliefs about God
founders of religions
sacred texts
worship and meditation
festivals
rites of passage
religious beliefs, ethical teachings and the rules of religions

It also cites examples of *key attitudes* that RE might be seen to encourage:

curiosity
self-confidence and esteem
respect for the views and ways of life of others
open-mindedness

Name: _____

what does God mean to you?

God Loves you and me
he is your and my Father
1 know that God is
the king of Kings and I
Would like to go to
heaven and when I am
in heaven I would like
to see God my Father.
I Think God is the best
thing. I Love God lik God Loves
me. I think God is White
because God is your and
my God. I know that there
is a lot of God. God is an man
I know God is an man
and I think God is big
I Love God.

Figure 2.1 What does God mean to you? Year 4, Hindu

Source: St George's Church of England Primary School, Birmingham

God means a lot because he made me
and every thing in the world. He
made Adam and Eve. He made families
and animals flowers and trees all
for us. I think that he's kind to me
and he is special. I kind of like
him so that's why I pray to him.
I think that he is a magic spirit
made from smoke. I think he is kind
and nice to me. He likes me. So I
like him a lot more than my mum dad
sister brother and baby. I like God
because he makes peace THE END.

Figure 2.2 What does God mean to you? Year 4, Muslim

Source: St George's Church of England Primary School, Birmingham

God means Love to me. Because he is
kind. In this world you have got
things that belong to god. I can not
see god. You will see god if you go
into space. There is one god. I can
trust god. I have a picture of god in
my head. I dream of god that he is
talking to me. I have prayed to god
lots of times in assembly. And god
means happiness with love. I think
god is big. I think god is 12 stones.
but I am not sure.

Figure 2.3 What does God mean to you? Year 4, Christian

Source: St George's Church of England Primary School, Birmingham

critical ability
consideration for others

Religious Education: A local curriculum framework reminds schools to use RE ATs and programmes of study to develop their curriculum plan for RE (p. 15). The plan might include: what should be taught to different year groups; key concepts and skills; how KS2 learning relates to KS1; pupil activities that relate to ATs and content and that provide evidence of attainment; appropriate learning experiences to the age and level of attainment of the child; a variety of teaching and learning methods; links with other subjects and cross-curricular themes.

Starting Out With the National Curriculum provides an advisory statement that could be described as foundation principles for *quality audit in RE* that:

- 'the quality of religious teaching should match that in other National Curriculum subjects'; and
- 'where appropriate, work in religious education should be assessed and reported'.

Schools might consider on a staff training day for RE how far their practice already matches this NC framework and what changes might be needed.

The NC documents therefore provide a framework within which to base further detailed RE planning at school level:

- within the local agreed syllabus structure and requirements; and
- in planning the use of RE content to meet ATs in other NC subjects.

This second can be one way of ensuring that RE is actually delivered in an already over-crowded primary curriculum. The following subjects are capable of having all their ATs approached via RE content:

English
Welsh first language
History
Art

Other subjects can have some of their ATs approached via RE content:

Maths AT1 (Reasoning, logic, proof strand), AT5 (Handling data – such as a survey of opinions, beliefs)
Science AT2 Life and living processes (strand on life processes and the organization of living things)
Welsh second language AT3, Writing (strands 1 to 3 esp. 3 expressing opinions)
Technology AT3, AT4 (Planning and making, Evaluating – using religious symbols, artefacts or buildings as starters)
Geography AT4 Human Geography (population settlements – religious and socio-economic influences)

Modern Foreign Languages – as part of recent experiments to teach 'subjects' through the medium of a modern foreign language, but also as a KS2 foundation for the PoS at KS3 and KS4 in I.4 'developing cultural awareness', II Area B Personal and Social Life. In the primary phase it may be important to be aware that 19 modern foreign languages count as NC languages.

Music AT2 Listening and appraising – when it is related to music from a religious tradition.

Even within Physical Education, where dance is one of three recommended out of six prescribed activities in KS1 and KS2, the exploration of a religious theme or story through this medium can be attempted.

As teachers are only too aware, NC ATs in some areas seem subject to constant change and the detail quoted above may already have been replaced. What matters more than the

KEY STAGE ONE

END OF KEY STAGE STATEMENTS	EXAMPLES
Drawing on Knowledge gained from the Programme of Study	
Pupils should be able to ...	**So that they could, for example ...**
A1 – begin to recognise examples of symbolic forms	talk about a story that has a meaning beyond the apparent e.g. The Tenth Good Thing About Barney.
A2 – be aware that beliefs, feelings and actions relating to God are the most important thing in life for some people	describe how regular daily prayers are important for Muslims.
A3 – be aware that some people belong to groups which are bounded by rules and customs	associate the wearing of the Five K's with a Sikh community.
B1 – be aware of the ways in which the value of every person is recognised	talk about the special place given to new born babies in Christian baptism.
B2 – recognise responses to the order and mystery of the world around them	talk about the way some people give thanks to God for the harvest
B3 – be aware that there are questions about life which many people find very puzzling	feel confident in talking about puzzling questions in their own and other people's experiences.
C – express their own feelings, reactions and responses in creative ways	draw a picture, make up a story or enact through play and expression of their own ideas and feelings.

Figure 2.4 Newham KS1 EKSS

detail, however, is the principle that RE content can service some NC ATs. Clearly RE content cannot replace prescribed programmes of study in each of these subjects. But it can underline and support them and where teachers are working from a topic bank to achieve various ATs they will be able to use RE programmes of study in the process.

The agreed syllabus will have its own ATs for RE. If so, these are as binding as ATs within other subjects and need to be built into the school's overall planning framework. An agreed syllabus might also have levels for RE. The earlier NC publication, *Religious Education: A local*

AGREED SYLLABUS: END OF KEY STAGE STATEMENTS

What follows is a statement of what might be achieved by the average pupil at the end of each Key Stage in relation to the two attainment targets.

KEY STAGE ONE

By the end of KEY STAGE ONE each pupil should:

RELIGIOUS LITERACY

Understand

that there is a sense of order, pattern, beauty and mystery in the natural world; know that a variety of people live in the local community and worship in different places; appreciate that some people, places, moments and things are special to each person; know some of the stories in the life of Jesus of Nazareth and at least one other principal religious leader; be able to show this by talking, drawing and/or writing about them.

Expressed

. . . through story, role-play, dance-drama, written and art work, personal experience and response.

SPIRITUAL DEVELOPMENT

Understand

the importance of building relationships, learning to trust each other and having confidence in their own abilities; appreciate that changes in the seasons affect changes in their lives and the lives of others; understand simple general principles which apply to behaviour and the consequences of particular behaviour; be able to show this by describing their observations and expressing their responses in a creative way.

Expressed

. . . through story, role-play, dance-drama, written and art work, personal experience and response.

Figure 2.5 Sefton KS1 EKSS

KEY STAGE

TWO

PROFILE COMPONENTS	MAP OF RELIGIOUS EDUCATION	OBJECTIVES	SKILLS	FOUNDATION UNITS
1 EXPLORING AND RESPONDING	A Communication and Interpretation of Religion	communicate imaginatively a religious belief, concern or issue of their own. / recognise and identify the central symbols of a religion and demonstrate some understanding of the meaning of this for believers. / consider the importance of authority. / demonstrate use of non-literal language, including religious language.	appreciating / participating / interpreting / experience / imagining / observing / responding / communicating / demonstrating / reflecting / considering / identifying	JESUS TAUGHT IN PARABLES THE BIRTHDAY OF THE WORLD Jewish Sabbath THE IMPORTANCE OF EASTER EID IL FITR
	B Celebration	describe in detail at least one major Christian festival. / demonstrate understanding of the difference between a fast, feast and celebration. / explore a festival from a faith other than their own.		
2 KNOWLEDGE AND UNDERSTANDING	C Lifestyle	be able to recount examples of religious codes of conduct. / show awareness of how religious communities and individuals express their obedience. / review the implications this might have for themselves.	examining	WHAT ARE COMMANDMENTS? JESUS' PRINCIPLES FOR LIVING RESPONSIBILITY "Love thy neighbour as thyself."
	D Belief and Values	know some of the ways in which religious people know and understand God. / know the names given to the followers of at least two religions and why these names are used. / understand some of the ways in which a believer expresses belief.	recounting / retelling in own words / knowing	THE FIVE PILLARS OF ISLAM THE QUR'AN
	E Worship and Practices	identify the principal features of worship in a chosen community. / research, record and analyse numbers, groups and types of people who use a religious building and how it is used. / undertake the study of a religious building within their own locality.	understanding / answering / describing / communicating	To be addressed during the final year of this Key Stage, i.e. Year 6 WHY DO PEOPLE FAST? Lent, Ramadan
	F Significant Figures and Events	identify the major events in the lives of key figures in Christianity and one other religion. / be able to give reasons as to why they are held in special regard by believers. / be able to name titles and roles of leaders of religious groups in the religions studied.	reviewing / investigating	WHAT DO CHURCHES TEACH? THE COMMERCIALISATION OF CHRISTMAS
3 AWARENESS OF LIFE EXPERIENCES AND OF QUESTIONS	G Ultimate Questions	know that there are many questions to which people give different answers, including questions about God. / be aware of some of the experiences which give rise to these questions.		
	H Natural World	show an understanding of religious views about the role of human beings in the natural world, their relationship to it and responsibility for it. / be familiar with some different attitudes and religious beliefs to death and life after death.	reflecting / imagining / responding / caring / showing respect / being sensitive / questioning / being aware / showing empathy	As with Key Stage One, visits and visitors are encouraged where possible

Figure 2.6 Newcastle upon Tyne KS2 map

STAGE 2 (7–11)

CONCEPTS	KNOWLEDGE	SKILLS	ATTITUDES	HUMAN EXPERIENCE
Beliefs: To deepen the child's understanding of God.	To study or to know about:	**Use of Language:** To begin to develop the ability to use and understand the language of religion.	**Responsible Relationships:** To appreciate that relationships involve response and responsibility.	**Spiritual Experiences:** To respond to spiritual experiences and to examine questions derived from human experience.
Importance of Religion: To recognise the importance of religion to believers.	**Sacred Writings:** Sacred Writings and their importance to believers.	**Use of Language:** To begin to develop the ability to explore different kinds of literature for example poetry, legend, parable and allegory.	**Integrity:** To value truth and be honest about one's feelings, attitudes and actions.	**Responsible Relationships:** To provide opportunities for children to appreciate that relationships involve a sensitive response and responsibility.
The Spiritual Dimension: To appreciate the meaning of a spiritual dimension to life.	**Sacred Writings:** Stories from the Bible in order to create a wider knowledge and understanding and to begin to develop a sense of chronology.	**Use of Sources:** To develop the ability to use a widening variety of primary and secondary sources.	**Enquiry:** To develop an enquiring approach to life generally and in particular to the fundamental and religious questions life poses.	**Emotions:** To appreciate the range of human experience as experienced by the children.
Commitment: To extend awareness that people commit themselves to God and respond in prayer, worship and service.	**Christian Teaching:** Significant elements of Christian teaching as contained in the Creed.	**Reasoned Argument:** To pose questions and seek reasoned answers.	**Social Awareness:** To develop an appreciation of the service, care and concern of others.	**Daily Experience:** To evaluate personal and shared experiences.
Commitment: To explore the influences of religious commitment on people's daily lives.	**Faith:** The effect of faith on the lifestyles of ordinary people.	**Empathy:** To develop the ability to enter imaginatively into the experiences of others.	**Social Responsibilities:** To develop an awareness of one's own capacity to contribute to the well-being of others in the family, school and community.	
Morality: To recognise and understand the difference between right and wrong.	**Founders of Faith:** The lives of founders of faith.	**Reflection:** To reflect upon one's own experiences and to consider those of others.	**Forgiveness:** To appreciate the need to give and receive forgiveness.	
Forgiveness: To appreciate the need to give and receive forgiveness.	**People of Faith:** The lives of outstanding people of faith and the actions of such people as expressions of faith.		**Sensitivity:** To show sensitivity towards, and develop an evaluative approach to religious beliefs, practices and institutions.	
Symbols: To begin to understand the significance of symbols.	**Prayer:** The meaning and formulation of prayer and the ways in which people pray including the Lord's Prayer.			
	Places of Worship: Places of worship of religious groups in the local and wider community.			

Morality: The Ten Commandments and the Sermon on the Mount and to be aware that all faiths have codes by which they live.

Customs and Celebrations: A widening range of religious customs and celebrations. Religious festivals and celebrations.

Symbolism: Some religious symbolism and ritual.

Tolerance: To develop a respect for people and their right to believe.

Ecological Responsibility: To develop a respect for the natural world as God's creation.

Ecological Responsibility: To develop a respect for the natural world as a place shared with fellow human beings.

Figure 2.7 Solihull KS2 map

curriculum framework (1991), noted that some agreed syllabuses were moving towards statements of attainment at ten levels not linked to key stages, devised on the basis that ability in RE is not always related to age. By March 1993, however, only two agreed syllabuses had prescribed levels but five had strands. For instance, in the Newham syllabus Attainment Target A, Knowing and Understanding, has the strands A1 Expressing Meaning, A2 Beliefs and Values and A3 Community, Tradition and Lifestyle while its AT B, Interpreting Questions, has the strands B1 Relationships, B2 Natural World and B3 Ultimate Questions. The 1993 NC document also noted different practice using a cluster of statements of attainment, all at the same level for each key stage, thus enabling the objectives to apply to a particular age group, but carrying the disadvantage that pupils would not have the opportunity to show higher attainment than that specified for their key stage (p. 8). The dominant trend in RE seems to be away from the attempted detail of levels and more in favour of an EKSS (End of Key Stage Statement) approach as in Art, Music and PE. In RE most EKSSs cluster around KS3 but the latest reported total for all key stages excluding 'KS5' (post 16) ranges from 28 to 160. Various ways of recording this in RE and presenting it for parents and pupils are being explored, but no single route has become the norm.

Sefton agreed syllabus (1992) adopted the ATs 1 Religious Literacy and 2 Spiritual Development. Their EKSSs for KS1 are shown in Figure 2.5.

The agreed syllabus will also provide a definition of key concepts, skills and attitudes and also programmes of study appropriate to each KS. The sample in Figure 2.6 is the KS2 map from the Newcastle upon Tyne agreed syllabus, reproduced by permission.

Solihull, in comparison, produced the map for KS2 RE (1991), shown in Figure 2.7, on p. 17 of their syllabus.

For RE, programmes of study and attainment targets are complementary, 'the one requiring what should be studied, the other setting required standards of work' (NCC, 1991, p. 9).

RE PLANNING AT CLASS LEVEL

When the class topics for the year have been identified – usually from the school topic bank and as a result of whole-school planning – the class teacher needs to decide whether any of these incorporate a natural rather than a forced RE dimension, and identify what this dimension might be and how it relates to the RE ATs and the ATs in other subjects. A topic on India would naturally suggest a dimension on Hinduism – or indeed other faiths – present in India. On the other hand a Science/Technology/History/Geography topic on Flight would not a have a natural RE dimension on angels, though this example is drawn from observed practice and not fiction!

This identification of RE content within the overall topic map for the academic year needs to be followed by the selection of appropriate RE-led topics. This should be at school level so that a coherent scheme is being followed in RE. The RE-led topics may have to meet RE ATs not covered by the other topics selected, or it may be that they are chosen in order to cover content required by the agreed syllabus. They may be delivered as integrated topics, like the others in every way except that the RE element is at the centre of the concept maps and planning grids rather than on the outside. Or they may be 'mini-topics', shorter than the possible half-term 'big' integrated topic and more subject specific. With the current tendency to emphasize subject teaching at the top end of KS2 one would certainly expect clearly identifiable RE topics to be in place there. But even within an integrated topic the RE element has to be identifiable for OFSTED inspection and to fulfil the 1988 ERA requirement. It cannot be claimed to be somehow invisibly present, like a lesser deity! One crude yardstick of quantity in RE is to check that it meets the minimum recommended annual hourage in the Dearing Report (4.20, p. 33) which is 36 (KS1) and 45 (KS2).

A class that had six half-term length 'big' topics per year, most of which embraced some aspects of RE, might reasonably be expected to include in addition at least four RE mini-topics in addition to the need to deal with Christmas and Easter. Christmas and Easter appear not merely because they are the main Christian festivals and contain within them interesting pre-Christian religious customs, but because they have become almost universal semi-secular festivals within our culture. Most people participate in Christmas and Easter to some degree by virtue of living in this culture: even atheists sing Christmas carols. Not only are Christmas cards now on sale from July – and until the sales the following February – but 'Easter' cream eggs and hot cross buns are available all the year round in our shops. Nor

Figure 2.8 Easter, March 1991. Finding the hidden eggs

Source: Cowick First School, Exeter. Photograph: Zoe Evans

should the repetition of Christmas and Easter as topics in RE in different key stages and classes be seen as an automatic disadvantage. Child maturation, progression and the wealth of available material to study make the repetition good sense – provided the planning shows clearly what is being done at which stage and how progression is expected to occur. 'What shall I do with my class for Christmas this year?' is a question born out of lack of RE planning for the school as a whole.

Having identified the RE-led topics and the RE element in other topics, the teacher needs to identify the key concepts, skills and attitudes and how they are to be achieved through the 'content', whether 'content' arises as a result of the use of video, visit, visitor, books or a programme of study from the agreed syllabus or supporting handbook etc.

The next step is to identify the methods of assessing, recording and reporting the RE that are to be employed. Again, this may be laid down in the agreed syllabus, but if not, a whole-school policy is essential.

Perhaps above all, the proper demands of the NC framework underline that RE must be planned and delivered as part of whole-school curriculum policies and not left to the enthusiasm or lack of it on the part of individual teachers about what if anything is to be delivered. That itself implies that in every school, someone on the staff must undertake to co-ordinate RE across the school. It may be that the person who volunteers or is 'selected' knows very little about RE, and in a small primary school that is quite likely to be the case. Staff development is then essential, and that might involve the following strategies, which are not to be seen as exclusive:

contacting the adviser or advisory teacher for RE;
contacting a SACRE teacher 'rep' to find out what INSET the SACRE has initiated;
undertaking one of the growing number of modular distance-learning courses in RE offered by universities or colleges of higher education which are self-standing or could lead with further course credits to a professional award (B.Phil, M.Ed, etc.).

   ACTIVITY 2.1

Planning priorities

If you are working in a school consider your possible priorities in planning RE:

the use of a training day or days
RE syllabus review
finding out about and acquiring new resources
updating the school policy statement on RE
planning RE into the yearly work of all classes
examining how RE content could help work towards non-RE ATs

What would be your two most urgent priorities? How could you start to meet them?

a ACTIVITY 2.2

RE and non-RE ATs

Assuming that you are not a trained RE specialist, go to the NC subject you know best and consider its ATs. Using your RE agreed syllabus can you identify areas of RE content within the KS you teach that could meet the ATs in your chosen subject? Choose a short enough sample area to be practicable to try as an experiment with your class.

Story and truth in RE

In our culture the idea of story has been debased: it has become something for children which adults have grown out of, or something known not to be true, as in the remark 'You're telling me a story.' Not surprisingly, children and sometimes adults persist in asking 'Is the story true?' when they really mean 'Is the story literally true?' Ironically, we tell stories all the time. 'A funny thing happened to me at school today' is rarely recounted as pure history! And the soaps of TV and radio provide endless storying from what is purported to be everyday life, from *The Archers* to *Neighbours* and the school-based soaps such as *Grange Hill*. Interestingly these soaps are often publicly rubbished by commentators and parodied by satirists yet many intelligent people watch them, even if a little guiltily. Is this perhaps a sign that we as adults are losing our ability to handle story? Arguably we need story just as much as humans have always done, yet in a literal and technological society we perhaps feel a need to scoff at it. It is ironic that the role of story in science is currently being acknowledged as a legitimate and vital means of communication. Story has a role in helping scientific enquiry, beginning with imaginative explanatory conjecture which then requires scrupulous analysis and testing.

 Scientists are building explanatory structures, *telling stories* [his italics] which are scrupulously tested to see if they are stories about real life.

(P. Medawar, *Pluto's Republic*, 1984, Oxford Paperback, p. 133)

Story is an art form in its own right, however, and can be analysed both in scientific and literary terms. Children can see truth in Aesop while handling the reality that the animals *they* know do not talk. They can see that though the good Samaritan is a figure in a story Jesus made up, the story carries other and deeper truths that do not depend on whether the Samaritan 'really' existed, whether we can trace his grave, his descendants or whatever. Getting children to ask what the truth is in the story matters more than their asking whether the story is true. For 'Did it happen?' is a more limiting and simplistic question than 'What's

Adam   and   EVE –   True   story   or   not

Christian
Y5

A man called God made the worldfor everybody.
He said "Adam and EVE Ive made this garden
for you but do not do one thing. Do not eat the
Fruit off one of the trees or else you will crinkle up
and die – If you do this you can blame yourself".
But one day when Eve was walking in the
Garden she heard the silent whispers of a
Snake "They Look nice apples dont they. Go ahead
and try one". Eve was so temted she took one.
Adam was with her and he ate one too
The months grew longer and they grew older
gradualy every day. Then in the month of febuary
the time had come and the end was near. They
gradualy passed away peacefully. God had warned
them and the snake that was tempting them was the
Devil. He wanted to destroy Gods Beautiful world.
but he never succeeded and thats why im here
today writing the story again. I like that story
it remminded me of a romantic couple who have
bought a nice house but they're not allowed
to eat the apples off their tree and they did
eat an apple and this story shows how disobedient
people can be especialy to our holy god the
Owner of the world. I would never do that, would
you? But Its one of the best stories ive ever heard.

Figure 3.1 Adam and Eve: how true? Year 5

Source: St George's Church of England Primary School, Birmingham

Adam and Eve — a true story or not?   Y5
J.W.

When God made The world He put animals there
and a man and weman called Adam and Eve. One day Eve
was by the Tree of Knowledge and a snake said to Eve
"if you eat from the tree of Knowledge you will be Like
God" so Eve told Adam and so Eve and Adam ate from
the tree and. God sent them out and in a few
years they died.

I Think the Story is true.
What I feel is that no one is perfect
and women and men do bad things
And the Bit that is the truth is
when God said that if you eat from the
tree of Knowledge you will Die and that did
happen.

Figure 3.2 Adam and Eve: how true? Year 5

Source: St George's Church of England Primary School, Birmingham

Adam and Eve-a true story? or not?   Y5
Christian

yes the Adam and Eve story is true about how
he made all the things now and Adam and
Eve lived in a garden called the garden of
Eden. and god says to not pick the tree of
knowledge and they didn't. so they lived happy
ever after. BUT .....when Adam was walking
past the tree a snake came out and told and
things went drastically wrong, and they were
sent out of the garden and then they grew old
and died.

WHAT YOU CAN LEARN.
remember that in the story we heard they
were very disobedient. and ate the fruit and
they were sent out the garden. If they obeyed
we could have lived forever, that shows
sometimes people are very disobedient.

Figure 3.3 Adam and Eve: how true? Year 5

Source: St George's Church of England Primary School, Birmingham

the truth or meaning?' That greed can damage people is a more important discovery than that dogs crossing bridges over streams with meat bones between their teeth may not in 'real' life pause to look at their reflection in the water. That the Jews explained their escape from Egypt as the saving act of God is more important than getting bogged down in whether the Red Sea waters parted vertically or whether it was a tidal estuary and the chariots got stuck in the incoming tide, interesting though that might be as a side issue.

Story is central to the great world faiths – the ultimate all-age, all-ability teaching technique – and these stories can be shared with children. That means for the teacher there is the twofold task:

to provide context, so that the story is understood against its original cultural or religious background and not just torn out of it;

to avoid turning religious stories into secular material by stripping out all the references to God, faith, religion, etc., for doing this destroys the material itself.

In the case of the good Samaritan, for example, it is important for children and adults to know who the Samaritans were, where they lived – there are still some 600 living descendants – their religious beliefs and law, why they and the Jews were 'daggers drawn', and why the religious expert who asked Jesus the question 'Who is my neighbour?' choked when Jesus asked him in reply who the neighbour was. Rather than name 'the Samaritan' he presumably muttered 'the one who showed him [the victim] kindness'. He was not going to name his traditional enemy as the doer of a good deed! (Luke 10.25–37). By not providing context for the story we may reduce it to merely a secular moral (Let's be nice to people) or create confusion by wrong association. Many children who have grown up on the good Samaritan story without the context being provided genuinely believe that this Samaritan belonged to an organization dedicated to helping desperate and suicidal people, instead of beginning to understand why that twentieth century organization arrived at its name. They resemble adults who have grown up assuming that the word Philistine means a cultural lout, a barbarian (itself a word with a history of misuse), without the background to know that the Philistines of the Bible had a rich and ancient culture, perhaps based on Cretan origins, certainly enhanced by their strong commercial base in iron manufacturing and their archaeological legacy of elaborate pottery.

Jonah, to take another example, is much more than an incredible but mildly amusing story about a man who ended up inside a big fish for three days. Incidentally, it was not a whale in the story, which itself illustrates the danger that we tell the story we want to hear and not what the actual story says. Of course, story tellers sometimes adapt a story in the telling, but if they are going to adapt it fairly they need to know both the story and its originating context. Otherwise – and this often occurs when the fish has become a whale – the story teller is not aware that they have altered the original. The Book of Jonah is about matters at the very heart of Jewish self-understanding: the nature of forgiveness and the issue of who exactly constitute God's people: the people of Israel or the enemy people of Nineveh or potentially all people. One group of teachers and RE researchers working on this have suggested telling it by use of three key words: salvation, prophet and repentance. So the class moves from *What did Jonah have to eat in the fish?* and *Did Jonah make the fish feel sick?* (6 year olds) to re-examine with the class Jonah's prayer from inside the fish (Jonah 2): 'In my distress, O Lord, I called to you and you answered me. From deep in the world of the dead I cried for help and you heard me. . . . The water came over me and choked me . . . and seaweed was wrapped round my head. . . . But you, O Lord, brought me back from the depths alive. . . . Salvation comes from the Lord.' Then child response includes such comments as:

It's saving!

Salvation means like you've been helped when you can't help yourself

and

When he was in the big fish he said a new sort of word

(6 and 7 year olds).

See the bibliography for this Unit, referring to *A Gift to the Child*.
So with story we can identify useful stages of teaching and learning;

1   The **communication** of the story, including its context, perhaps with appropriate class-room ritual – lighting a story candle, seating children around us, going to the story corner, starting with a stilling exercise such as the Buddhist suggestion of listening for the most distant sound, or even waiting until the class can hear a real pin drop! This telling the story as it is, allowing the children to reflect imaginatively upon it, is the basis for all development of story. By doing this accurately the story teller has not provided 'false' information which the child has to unlearn later, but *has* supported the child by re-telling the story in its framework as a basis for later consideration of what the 'truth' element is.

2   Seeing ourselves as **looking in** on the story (*Jonah believed God was speaking* rather than *I am telling you that God was speaking to Jonah*, which implies that there is no shadow of objective doubt about God and I am requiring you to believe in him as essential to this exercise).

3   The **questions** we want to ask – providing time for children to raise issues and being ready to push some questions back (*Well, what do you think about that?*).

4   Our **imaginative entering** into aspects of the story: what would it be like for . . . or if. . . . How might she have felt when . . . ? Should they be doing X or Y or Z?

5   We pick out **key words** in the story; if 'hibernate' or 'extinct' is possible in infant science or 'pyramid' or 'cuboid' in infant maths, then 'prophet' is equally possible in religious education. 'Prophet' would certainly be worth using as it is a key concept in three faiths – Judaism, Christianity and Islam. Not being able to spell it – profit and phrophet still abound – does not mean not being able to understand or say something about it.

6   The **beliefs** of the people in the story and the people who passed it on become clearer as the child passes through the first five stages.

7   We **think about our beliefs** (secular and religious) in relation to the themes of the story:

treatment of animals, forgiveness, care for the earth, etc.

8   We **re-tell or express the story** in other ways: 1, 4, 6 or 7 – follow-up discussion or drama or display or dance or mime?

Merely telling it and then getting children to draw a picture is a waste of a good story, because it fails to explore it properly.

ACTIVITY 3.1

Turning a religious story into good RE

Choose any religious story you know.

1   Investigate its context by using a Bible dictionary or commentary or an appropriate background book for the faith your story comes from.

2   Read it if you can in the original scripture or book, to get nearer to what the writer wanted to convey than using a paraphrase or adapted children's version.

3   Sum up in a sentence the beliefs of the people in the story and those of the people who passed it on.

4   Identify one or two key words to understanding the theme of the story, words that you would want your children to use and understand.

5   Now you have a basic framework, check and structure the story against the categories above, being careful to check that you do not edit out references to 'God' on grounds of supposed difficulty etc.

6   Try it with a class or group of children and then compare what you have achieved with your previous use of story in RE. Has it helped you and the children to go deeper?

If you are 'stuck' for a story, try the Jewish and Christian Bible story of Ruth in the Bible book of that name. Context requires an understanding of the custom of 'Levirate' marriage, that if a man died childless and had a brother, he was required to marry the widow to raise children to keep the family name going (see Deuteronomy 25.5–10). Boaz goes further than the law requires. One of the strikingly modern themes is racial harmony. One of the obvious section 7 contrasts to make with our society is the position of women. One of the writer's religious themes is the reliability of God. Another belief of the writer is that even David, the ideal Jewish king, has Moabite ancestry and that despite some Jewish exclusiveness (see Ezra 10 and Nehemiah 13.25–27) God finds acceptable some of those outside the Jewish community. The best Bible translations use the word 'redeem' rather than 'buy' for the field in Ruth 4.4. This could be a key word in the story to establish with children because it can relate to later exploration of redemption as a key word in Christianity.

Or try this story from two religions of the east. It is told in Hinduism and Buddhism. Once upon a time a beautiful and well-dressed woman visited a house.

The owner of the house asked her who she was and she replied that she was Lakshmi, the goddess of wealth. The owner was delighted and he treated her extremely politely and gave her presents and food. Soon after, another woman appeared who was ugly and old and poorly dressed. The owner asked who she was and she told him that she was the goddess of poverty. The owner was frightened when he knew this and tried to get rid of her from his house – he wanted no poverty there! But she refused to leave and told him that the goddess of wealth was her sister. 'We have an agreement never to live separately', she told him, 'if you chase me out, she leaves too.' But he still did not want Poverty in his house. Sure enough, the old woman disappeared and her sister went with her.

Context requires that this be told in one of its religious frameworks. *The Teaching of Buddha* (see Bibliography, Unit 4) includes it in a section of (already) ancient fables in a chapter on the Way of Purification, itself part of a section on Practice. The text continues (Practice, I 3.12): 'Birth goes with death. Fortune goes with misfortune. Bad things follow good things. People should realise this. Foolish people dread misfortune and strive after good fortune, but those who seek Enlightenment must rise above both of them and be free of worldly attachments.' Key words and phrases from this Buddhist version would be 'rise above' (transcend) and Enlightenment. Changed cultural context means that we must also consider the question of strangers at the door – men or women. In a modern context in which we are constantly emphasizing don't answer the door if your parents are out, don't speak to strangers, etc., this story cannot simply be told without contextual help about ancient hospitality.

 ACTIVITY 3.2

Story in a changed cultural context

Stories arise in a particular cultural context, and the best are able to survive the disappearance of their originating context. This can have the effect of making them seem alien in a different culture and time. One example of this is the story of Abraham's willingness to sacrifice Isaac (Genesis 22), or Ibrahim and Ishmael as it is in the Islamic tradition. Popular as this story still is in some primary RE, the difficulty is that re-told in our late twentieth century western culture it can look almost like an intended ritual child abuse. In this case it might be better to defer the story altogether until the child is older and can understand more of the context.

Or to take another example, the tiny cameo incident – for this purports to be history – of Jesus' encounter with Martha and Mary (Luke 10.38–42) can easily be made to look like a conscientious, hard-working, busy person being valued less than a 'scatty' dreamer. But is it that? Read the account for yourself and decide how you would tell it. It may have had several cultural contexts in the course of its transmission. One scholar (Laland) suggests it might have been re-told by Luke in his contemporary context of the expanding young churches to offer guidance for entertaining visiting missionaries: offer them simple fare and take time to listen to what they say! Another New Testament scholar, Howard Marshall, points out that the implication of the Greek language in Luke's telling of the story is that Martha wished to hear Jesus, but was prevented by the pressure of providing hospitality, wishing to honour him with an elaborate meal. The Aramaic word for Martha is Mar, which means the mistress of the house. More importantly, Marshall points out that the key to this incident lies in its contemporary Jewish context of the role of women. Women were discouraged from learning and engaging in discourse with rabbis for reasons of propriety. What by implication Jesus is doing here – and there is evidence elsewhere in this same gospel that his approach to women was unconventional, direct and affirmative – is to give women a place above domestic chores in the listening and learning within the spiritual life of the group. In this sense he is affirming the first Jewish commandment: put God first (Deuteronomy 5) – the meal can wait.

Muhammad's support for polygamy can be made to look appallingly sexist in late twentieth century re-telling, but in the historical and cultural context of the tribal society of his day he was raising the dignity and position of women from that of property to that of person.

Clearly primary teachers cannot be expected to have an encyclopaedic knowledge of the cultural context of the stories they may be re-telling across a range of faiths. But they can use a simple checklist of preparation to ensure that they do not damage a story – and therefore the child's understanding of it – in the re-telling. They need to

- feel sufficiently conversant with the religious tradition in broad terms to feel confident to re-tell the story from it;
- have access to interpretative material about the story – commentaries, background books – to uncover any lost clues to understanding it that need to be built into their presentation for children;
- avoid editing out the religious references in the re-telling of the story to make it fit increasingly secular western culture. Joseph without God in the story is really a project on aspects of ancient Egypt and not RE at all.

 ACTIVITY 3.3

Story emphases in RE

A long, long time ago, Onyankopon lived on the earth and was always very close to people. They liked that. There was a little old woman who used to pound her mashed yams in a great wooden bowl – thump, thump, grind, grind – but the pestle she was stirring with kept knocking up against Onyankopon because he was so close. Thump, thump, grind, grind, stir, stir, – ouch! But she kept on doing it. Thump, thump, grind, grind, stir, stir – ouch! Still the old woman kept on pounding her mashed yams. Finally Onyankopon said angrily to her 'Why do you keep on with your thump, thump, grind, grind, stir, stir – you keep hurting me. Because of that I'm going away up into the sky.' And that is exactly what he did. He disappeared.

So people weren't close to him any more and they were sad because they wanted his advice and they wanted him to be their friend. It was the old woman who thought of a way to reach him and bring him back for the people. She told the children to go and search for all the mortars they could find and bring them to her. Then she told them to pile one mortar on top of another until they built the stack high enough to reach where Onyankopon was. They tried it. The children of the village went and found all the mortars they could lay their hands on and brought them to her. She stacked them up one on top of another until they could almost reach the place where Onyankopon was. Up and up and up went the stack of mortars – but they were just one mortar short. Not quite there. The children went and searched and asked and looked and looked. But they couldn't find a single extra mortar anywhere. So they came and told the old woman. 'It won't work. We're one mortar short.' She said to them 'Don't worry. It's simple. Take one mortar out from the bottom of the pile and put it on the top – then we can reach Onyankopon.' So the children took one mortar out from the bottom of the pile – and the whole heap crashed to the ground harming many people. And they never did get close to Onyankopon again.

(Ashanti tribal story)

What points would you want to emphasize in using this story in RE? To compare your answer with mine, go to Appendix III on p. 90.

ACTIVITY 3.4

Story telling

If story is an art form, perhaps story telling is a craft! We must assume that despite the figure of speech, there is no such thing as a 'born story teller' for no baby has yet been born telling gripping tales of the journey down the birth canal. It therefore follows that story telling involves acquirable skills. From reflection on your own story telling and that of your colleagues, in class, assembly, etc., identify some of the skills that a good story teller demonstrates and isolate one or two of those that you could work on to build into or improve on in your own practice. Consider as examples the use of facial expression, or of pause, or the use of repetition to underline a point, especially with very young children to whom stories of the Chicken Licken type will have a special appeal.

ACTIVITY 3.5

Less literate children and story

Can children with low writing and spelling skills but high oracy excel in the telling or the understanding of story?

How can this hypothesis be verified? If you have a primary class devise a simple experiment to see if this is so. In what ways should teachers be building on this capacity to understand story in their daily work with the less literate child?

ACTIVITY 3.6

Children's understanding

Ronald Goldman wrote two books in the 1960s that exerted a major influence over primary RE for decades. In one he wrote:

> The greatest danger for the Infant pupil is that of acquiring a religious vocabulary which has no conceptual substance, comparable to possessing a number vocabulary without number insights.
>
> (*Religious Thinking from Childhood to Adolescence*, 1964, Routledge, London, p. 232)

But while the understanding and acquiring of religious vocabulary matters towards developing an understanding of religious concepts, children also seem capable of intuitive understanding of story, even where they lack the vocabulary to articulate this understanding. How important do you think a 'religious vocabulary' should be, compared with, say, a historical vocabulary or the mathematical vocabulary to which Goldman refers?

ACTIVITY 3.7

Assessing children's understanding of story

How do we know if a child has understood a story? Goldman (see above) in his research tried to explore how far children had understood various stories which were then in common use in RE. One was the story of Moses at the burning bush (Exodus 3.1–6). Goldman asked his sample of children why they thought the ground on which Moses stood was holy. The answers he received included:

Because there was grass on it. (A throw back to KEEP OFF THE GRASS?)
He was standing on a ho.
It was hot ground. It would burn his shoes.
Because God blessed it.
It was where God was standing.

Of course, these were answers to a prepared set of questions and not the result of a guided exploration of the story with the teacher. But is Moses at the bush a suitable story for (a) infants or (b) juniors or (c) best left to secondary school, if told at all? Why? Why not? If you were to tell it, what questions would you ask in order to see whether the children had understood it? Is there a 'right' answer to these questions?

a   ACTIVITY 3.8

Types of story

Adults recognize and try to classify particular types of story: history; legend; fable; the unhappily defined category 'myth' and that special form of religious riddle so often ruined by moralizing interpretations, parable.

How far is it useful to help older juniors to start to see some of these categories? Which would be your priorities for them to understand?

Before discussing myth with children, how would you define myth for the teacher? Would it be adequate to describe it as 'a story told as a vehicle of religious or moral insight or truth'? That would imply that the religious or moral truth might stand irrespective of the historical or scientific truth of the story.

Unit 4

Exploring world religions

Do I completely understand the faith I am about to teach?

Can I teach a faith in such a way that children gain a complete understanding of it?

If these are assumed to be the qualifications required to teach a world religion and the anticipated outcome, all teachers would be bound to fail. But if we set the more realistic and limited questions

Can I teach one or two aspects I understand fairly well about a faith in such a way that the children can understand them?

and

Could a member of that faith see themself in what is being taught and learned?

we are on surer ground.

The six faiths most commonly referred to in RE syllabuses are Hinduism, Buddhism, Judaism, Christianity, Islam and Sikhism. Fortunately it is not suggested that they should all be taught every year to every child in equal depth! Within these faiths the study of some topics, like Christmas, might recur annually. Others might not recur at all. Some topics benefit from a re-visit as children mature, while others, though perhaps interesting to children, are not perhaps central to the faith being studied and do not require repetition.

It is in this area of world faith work that many teachers feel at their most inadequate, for very few primary teachers have been trained in depth in world faiths unless they happen to be RE specialists. Even the specialists will rarely have studied all six world faiths above in depth, so their lack of knowledge about a particular faith the syllabus requires to be taught might be just as great as that of the non-specialist teacher. This could be one area in which to ask a SACRE to lobby for INSET provision. Getting the right resource material has to be the priority, since all teachers are under massive constraints on their time for planning. The thumbnail guide to resource material is to check to see whether what you are looking at has been written by a member of the faith it deals with or in consultation with members of that faith. Of course, that does not make it automatically suitable for every – or even any! – group of children, but the non-specialist teacher's professional judgement will deal with this issue of presentation and adaptation to their class more easily than with the nature and selection of the material from the faith itself. Of course teachers may touch on faiths other than the six listed: Zoroastrianism (with its possible links with the wise men and Christmas), Jainism, Baha'i, Shinto, etc. More likely, however, than an excursion into less well-known religions is that as part of topic work a class or group may be dealing with 'extinct' or 'deceased' faiths such as the religion of ancient Egypt or of Greece or Rome. In the case of these 'dead' faiths the questions to set against the way in which we present them are different from the ones used above:

Have I made the faiths or their members look puerile or stupid or 'primitive' in the derogatory sense, by telling their stories without interpretation (e.g. that the ancient Egyptians 'believed' that a scarab beetle pushed Ra, the Sun, across the sky). This danger is not restricted to extinct faiths. It can express itself in comments such as 'Hindus worship statues' when the Hindu view is that the god is in the statue, that the statue embodies the god's presence, but Hindus are perfectly well aware that the statue is manufactured – and eventually disposed of – by humans. With a living faith there are members of it around who can point this out; with 'extinct' faiths it is harder to check.

Has the idea of story as a vehicle for belief or value been sufficiently emphasized? For example, in telling the story that Ra sneezed and in the expectorated contents of his mouth shot out the earth, have children understood this as a powerful and vivid means of suggesting the accidental/chance origins of the earth and its vile nature, or have they been left with a 'yukky' story which is 'untrue' and even stupid because they have assumed it is to be believed or disbelieved literally?

Have the children been involved in the same sort of detective work as archaeologists are in trying to reconstruct the beliefs of prehistoric peoples using non-written evidence? (Why do you think they were buried with food and weapons? What might the plan of this building suggest it was used for? Why might this be a statue of a god? What is the evidence here for animal sacrifice? Why might it have been done? And so on. This of course addresses History AT2 as well.)

The final question teachers need to address in their RE work in world religions over a year is:

Have I got the balance right in faiths we have studied this year?

Or did the topic on ancient Egypt prove such a success that the friezes and the topic books and the plays and the writing fill nearly all the RE time and leave the impression that religion was vital a long time ago, but that it is dead now? Or did the teacher's enthusiasms for Sikhism and the devotion of an entire year's RE work to it, much as the children enjoyed it, address the situation of that class, living on a Scottish island, with Sikhs no nearer than Glasgow? Or did they do that at the expense of the PoS from the agreed syllabus?

This is a way of stating that one vital component in the selection of material is the **composition of the class, as well as the more obvious factor of its age**. Some classes will be a mixture of children from committed Christian families with regular and active church links, from families that consider themselves to be Christian, but with less (if any) church links (perhaps Christmas midnight mass or harvest festival), and children from families with no particular link and varying from indifference to hostility towards institutional or 'church' Christianity. This sort of class is often misleadingly thought of as monochrome, white, often rural and Christian! Other classes will contain children from different ethnic backgrounds and from different faiths. In such classes children from practising Christian families may be in a minority – just as they are in reality in the so-called white, Christian classes. More significantly, children from another practising faith background such as Islam may predominate. Teachers can expect to find varying degrees of commitment within families in any religion, just as they do among the families that think of themselves as Christian, though the percentage of those actively involved in the religious institutions of non-Christian religions may be higher. Put another way, the percentage of non-practising Muslims may be lower than the percentage of non-practising Christians. We should not treat, say, all children from Muslim homes as experts on their faith. Indeed, religious leaders are sometimes embarrassed when well-meaning school teachers in an attempt to affirm the religious and cultural background of children in their class ask them questions about their faith which they cannot answer, having not reached that point yet in their studies at mosque or religion school or their equivalent. It would be a mistake to assume any child is an expert in a faith simply by virtue of being brought up in it. It is also important to be aware that there are varieties of practice in most world faiths and it can be misleading to say 'All Sikhs believe.... All Muslim women wear ...' etc. In this sensitive situation teachers may feel uncertain as to what content to choose for their RE. In deriving this, these factors should be taken into account:

the requirements of the agreed syllabus and the advice in any accompanying handbook;
the 'global village' with its implied requirement that we should know about different faiths in order to understand one another better, to promote tolerance and celebrate diversity;
the UK with its Christian cultural inheritance and with Christianity as the largest practising faith group within it, with the implied requirement that all its citizens should have some understanding of this faith and the part it has played in shaping the country and its culture;
the classroom setting, including the actual faiths represented within it, with the implied requirement that in teaching we shall attempt to affirm all children in their background and let them extend their knowledge and understanding of others, again celebrating diversity rather than pretending that all religions or all people are the same.

Bearing in mind these four factors teachers will derive the schemes of work for a particular school or class. Which religions will be studied, and for how long in terms of time allocation for each, will also arise out of consideration of these issues, but they will not be necessarily the same percentage time per religion, nor per school, even within neighbouring schools, for family faith backgrounds may be different even within a small locality. However, the recent trend in agreed syllabuses is to be quite clear on the balance required and that must be regarded as the dominant factor.

Presenting aspects of several faiths means that the teacher is not concerned to promote any one of these faiths as more right or more true or 'better' than the others. Nor should it be seen as a facile window shopping between faiths, for few adults, let alone children, are ever in a position to choose between faiths. The 'choice' most adults face is between the faith of their family or upbringing – if they had one – and agnosticism or atheism. Rather the teacher has to present these faiths as part of the world – and UK – we all inhabit, and all held with sincerity by their believers, influencing their family life, moral values, life-style, etc. That does not mean that truth questions have to be swept under the carpet like infant questions about Father Christmas! Teaching world religions is not the same as saying they are all equally 'true'. What constitutes the 'truth' is what growing children – and adults – have to decide for themselves.

Consider this junior class discussion after an assembly about Easter:

   Child A comes from a practising Christian family, B from a practising Muslim family, C from no particular affiliation.

A.   *Being nailed must have been horrible.*
B.   *Mmm.*
A.   *Perhaps he didn't feel it.*
C.   *Didn't feel it?*
A.   *Being God's son, I mean, he might not have felt it.*
C.   *I don't see how God can have a son.*
B.   *He can't. He doesn't need one. Allah's, like, complete.... On his own.*
A.   *No, God sent his son, for us.*

All this is going well, as a discussion on how literally you take religious language, on the Muslim view that God neither has nor needs children and the Christian view that Jesus was God incarnate, God in a human form, until C has a brain wave:

C.   *Miss, come over here a minute, please.* [She does.] *How can God have a son?*

What would you say in reply? To compare your response to others, refer to Appendix III, p. 90.

These are some of the issues and principles in tackling world faiths. The activities that follow are attempts to deal with them in practice.

ACTIVITY 4.1

The artefact route

Obtain a religious artefact from one of the following: the public library schools' service, museum service, local secondary school RE department, a local religious community, a family in school who practise that religion, or a retail outlet such as the one listed in the Bibliography.

Find out about its history and symbolism – many artefacts come with accompanying leaflets or handbooks – and how it is used today by members of that religion.

Show it and tell its story to the class or group. Then get some of them to do the follow-up research to find its background in more detail, so that it becomes a window into that religion for further study.

Examples: a Hindu god statue; a Muslim prayer mat; a Jewish tallit; the Sikh five 'Ks'; a Buddha statue; a piece of matzah (many supermarkets sell them in the plural matzot on the cream cracker shelf); Muslim subha beads; a Jewish Torah scroll; a Hindu arti tray prepared for the arti ceremony; a Jewish seder dish.

An RE artefact corner or display in the classroom can then be established and changed or added to periodically. I have been fortunate to have on occasions parents whose job has taken them abroad. They are often willing to obtain – and even donate! – religious artefacts from the countries in which they have worked.

Other vital windows into religions for teachers and pupils alike are through visits and visitors, for each person can learn at their level from the occasion. A visitor might be asked in advance to prepare to tell the class one short story from their religion that means a lot to them and that might interest the class as a way into studying further. Visits and visitors are dealt with further in Unit 7. Take care, for the wrong person showing 5000 slides of their visit to Israel can be just as damaging as the wrong one showing 5000 slides of their holiday anywhere else!

ACTIVITY 4.2

Learning with the pupils

Select a religion you know very little about and over a period of time from the school and public libraries collect a group of half a dozen or more books or booklets, for children or adults, about this religion. When you have borrowed this small collection, **set aside the books**, or bookmark the sections that are likely to interest primary children in your class most:

daily and family life – food requirements, religious clothing, religious observances in the home;

growing up as a child in whatever religion you are exploring;
holy days and community gatherings for worship, social exchange, etc.;
special places and buildings;
special people such as the founder of the religion or some of its heroines and heroes;
special actions to celebrate the birth of a baby, or joining the group;
special journeys, e.g. pilgrimage;
special beliefs;
how the religion began.

This might seem to be everything about the religion rather than a selection, but in fact even a collection of books rather than a single book may not yield information on some of these areas and some of the books for adults concentrate strongly on the beliefs and philosophy of the different religions at the expense of the other aspects which children find more helpful and interesting as a way in.

Eliminate all the material that has no associated pictures; even the most able primary child will make little sense of a religion they know nothing of if they cannot see some of its practice. If you are worried about eliminating this, consider this incident I saw on a teaching practice visit: as part of RE work on Judaism the student drew on the blackboard a tallit (Jewish prayer shawl) which the children were asked to copy into their file. It was drawn in white chalk on the black board, not particularly well. The children were neither shown a real tallit, nor even a photograph of one. What was this exercise worth, since after some ten minutes of drawing they had merely a copy of the student's poor drawing from memory of a tallit?

Having eliminated from your collection of material what is unsuitable, structure a draft worksheet to take a child reader through the aspects of the religion you have selected as interesting and important and relevant to other ongoing work in other NC subjects. Try the worksheet on an individual or group when the rest of the class is engaged on group work activities. From the individual or group's progress through this and their questions, you will be ready to **revise and extend** your material, revising the worksheet and acquiring new books or artefacts as you extend your range. In this way you will have produced material that can be extended across the whole class and started to extend your own understanding of the faith in question.

Exploring Christianity

Could it be that the worst taught faith in RE is Christianity, because we are so culturally entangled in it?

DES Letter 3/89 highlights the requirement of the Education Reform Act (1988) that all new syllabuses – from 29 September 1989 onwards – must 'reflect the fact that the religious traditions in Great Britain are in the main Christian' (26.(i), p. 9).

The place of world faiths in RE was examined in Unit 4 but certainly the current cultural reality is that in the western world Christianity is still the dominant religion, whether we personally happen to believe in it or not. The educational reasons, therefore, for teaching Christianity are to do with youngsters understanding their own cultural roots and heritage and also understanding something of what it means to take a faith seriously, by learning about the western world's leading living faith. As we have suggested, for most youngsters the long term choice into adulthood is whether to be a member of the faith of their culture or family or whether to be an agnostic or an atheist or a humanist. Few adults, let alone children, are ever in a position to choose between faiths. So the long term choice for many youngsters is not whether to be a Sikh or a Muslim or a Hindu or a Christian, but whether to be a Christian (or whatever is the faith of their culture or family) or an agnostic or an atheist. But extra problems can arise because we are all culturally entangled in Christianity. For instance, is Christmas a Christian festival or not? Are we Christian by virtue of participating in it? Or are we Christian because we live in a 'Christian country' or at least one whose language and literature and law and architecture have been greatly influenced by Biblical–Christian stories and ideas? What or who is a Christian and why does the question seem so much harder to answer than defining a Muslim or a Sikh?

Who has the right to define Christianity authoritatively? Even the Bible does not provide a clear definition. What does it mean that some people indicate themselves as 'C of E' on hospital admission forms or affirm their C of E identity by going to church for 'hatch–match–dispatch' (christenings, marriage, funerals) and at no other times? Why do non-church-going adults and children sometimes talk about 'our religion' or 'our Bible' in conversation with those of other faiths? Who is the 'we' or 'us'? Why do many older primary children still confusingly try to distinguish between 'Christians' and 'Catholics'? And why does primary school work on Christianity so often appear to equate it with the C of E and the parish church or cathedral visit, when the Christian presence, even in the UK, reflects far more diversity? None of these questions might have universally agreed answers, but the mere fact that they arise in the context of teaching Christianity in any primary school illustrates the confusion within or brought about by our culture and its Christian legacy.

ACTIVITY 5.1

The diversity of Christianity

1   What have the following in common: Moravians; the Countess of Huntingdon's Connexion; Christadelphians; Wesleyan Reform?
    Go to Appendix III p. 90 to check your answer.

2   Can you name the various Christian groups or denominations that are represented in your school?

ACTIVITY 5.2

Disentangling Christianity from its western cultural setting

Are there any distinctive patterns of belief or behaviour that enable us to distinguish Christians from non-Christians in our society? The items in the opinionnaire that follows were supplied by KS4 children, based on their perceptions of what being a Christian involves. They then used it on their contemporaries to generate debate about what a Christian is and entails. It could equally be used by teachers themselves in an effort to distinguish Christianity from its western cultural setting.

What would its counterpart for Key Stage 2 look like? Work on one by children could also meet Maths AT5.

What difference should being a Christian make?

Opinionnaire: 1 = Agree strongly; 3 = Don't know; 5 = Disagree strongly. Circle your choice and be ready to defend it to the group !

A Christian should

(a) work hard at school or home	1	2	3	4	5
(b) go to church regularly	1	2	3	4	5
(c) pray regularly	1	2	3	4	5
(d) give generously to charities	1	2	3	4	5
(e) read the Bible sometimes	1	2	3	4	5
(f) be ready to help other people	1	2	3	4	5
(g) try to follow Jesus' example	1	2	3	4	5

A Christian should *not*

(h) deliberately set out to get drunk	1	2	3	4	5
(i) swear	1	2	3	4	5
(j) live immorally	1	2	3	4	5
(k) tell lies	1	2	3	4	5
(l) steal	1	2	3	4	5
(m) smoke	1	2	3	4	5

 ACTIVITY 5.3

Who is a Christian?

1   Ask your children who or what they think a Christian is. If they are not writing their answers, recording their responses on tape may help analyse types of response later.

2   Then looking at their answers, or listening to their tape, do you detect unity or

variety; clarity or confusion? Can you account for what you find in your sample?

3   In a society in which regular church goers are a minority, where do you think your children are getting their ideas on this subject? How far do you think these Bible advices have shaped the views of children who have probably never read or heard them directly?

Do not steal (Exodus 20.15)

Do not accuse anyone falsely (Exodus 20.16)

An eye for an eye, a tooth for a tooth (Deuteronomy 19.21, Exodus 21.24, Leviticus 24.20)

Do for others what you want them to do for you (Matthew 7.12)

Don't you know that your body is the temple of the Holy Spirit? (I Corinthians 6.19)

There is more happiness in giving than in receiving (Acts 20.35)

The love of money is a root of all kinds of evil (I Timothy 6.10)

HOW TO EXPLORE CHRISTIANITY LOCALLY

In planning a lesson to show something of the diverse nature of Christianity in the local environment, we need to select illustrative material. Here is the basis of display material collected by a PGCE student:

one example of a church that has a high degree of visual symbolism, so that children can see the richness of symbolism in Christianity, and how it is used by worshippers. Therefore an Anglican church (in England = the Church of England) or a Roman Catholic church or an Orthodox Church will provide a good example.

one example of a church that for religious reasons has deliberately restricted its visual symbolism so that worship may be more 'pure' or 'simple', or aural. A Methodist church, or a United Reformed, or Pentecostal or Baptist church or Church of Scotland (Presbyterian) would provide a good example – the best being the Baptist or Pentecostal church if they are willing to show children the baptistry, often a tank in the floor in which believers, never babies, are baptized by total immersion.

one example of a worshipping group that helps to establish the notion that the church is not an empty building nor even a building at all, but a worshipping community. A house church group or a group using, say, a local community centre for their worship, provides a photographic reminder that to Christians the church is neither a museum nor a shell – nor cold, as church buildings often seem to children on weekday visits when there's no heating on!

a   ACTIVITY 5.4

Tooling up for work on Christianity locally

This can be a very good use of all or part of a training day or for students on school-based work or teaching practice to undertake for themselves and on behalf of their school.

Make arrangements to visit places of Christian worship near your school and take a series of photographs or a video of the outside and inside of the buildings, focusing on special or prominent objects: pulpits, altars, lecterns, crucifixes, stations of the cross, fonts, candles, etc. At the same time obtain information about what that group does during the week: magazines, noticeboards, posters, etc., provide evidence that the group is more than just a Sunday meeting.

---

a   ACTIVITY 5.5

What do vicars do all day?!

This is an activity to do with children.

Jokes are still trotted out to the effect that the clergy have a one day working week, Sunday, but most people are unaware of what their real working life does entail, so that the rather stereotypical image of the vicar still exists. Invite a member of the local clergy, chosen not for their denomination but for their capacity to interest children, and with your class interview them about a week in their working life. They may be willing to go through their diary for a typical week. Children are invariably surprised by what they hear and it provides them with a clearer view of the role of the clergy in Christianity. It may lead into work using bar charts etc. to plot the amount of time spent on different activities: leading worship, visiting, work with youth, study, etc. It may lead into a reporter from the class or a group accompanying the member of the clergy for all or part of a day. The children will have to plan before the interview with the clergyman or woman what questions they want to ask.

NOTE

Despite the popular use of the word vicar to mean a member of the Christian clergy, accurate use of the word relates it to a particular job within the Church of England and there to be distinguished from other jobs such as curate, archdeacon, rural dean, etc. It can be hurtful to people to mislabel them, and although primary school children may not understand the theological reasons for the different terms in use among the clergy, it is important to introduce the visitor as whatever she or he is: the vicar or minister or priest or pastor or officer (Salvation Army) or whatever the appropriate term is. If in doubt, ask!

The ungrammatical phrase 'the Reverend Smith' as opposed to the Reverend Fred Smith or the Reverend Mr Smith has also gained ground massively, even in the BBC! But Reverend is a title (= worthy of reverence or respect) and Reverend Smith makes as little sense as loving Smith or kind Smith.

ACTIVITY 5.6

Exploring Christian diversity within the locality

This is an activity to do with older primary children and might follow on from or contrast with something like a parish church visit.

Invite a member of the Salvation Army (the officers are their full time staff, comparable with clergy in the other denominations, 'promotion' depending on length of service) to come in uniform to visit the class. In setting up the interview there are various areas to choose from in planning questions:

the symbolism of the uniform and the flag;
the early days of the Army and General Booth;
services now, including weddings and funerals;
what the Army does in its caring role;
Salvationist beliefs.

Or invite a local Quaker.

Quakerism dispels church stereotypes by not having clergy or set services or hymns or sermons or visual images like candles, crosses, etc. In its tradition that God can speak directly to the listening person, and that there is 'something of God' in every person, Quakerism takes a simple, sometimes shocking, approach to Christian expression of belief and worship. In setting up the interview choose from these possible areas:

What happens in Quaker 'meetings', as their services are called?
Why do they have 'meeting houses' not churches?
Quaker weddings and funerals.
How Quakers started and why George Fox kept his hat on!
What Quakers do to work for peace and why it matters to them.

Older primary children find it a thought-provoking contrast to their expectations derived from other church visits or visitors.

In both cases it is important to plan how much pre-visitor and how much post-visitor work needs to be done to get the best value out of the visit itself. Children will need help in preparing questions appropriate to the visitor and occasionally need guidance on what is socially appropriate too. 'How much do you get paid?' may produce laughter, shock or frosty horror on the part of an interviewee! Asking the class or group at preparation stage why we ought not to ask the visitor how much they get paid can be a useful exercise in *ad hoc* PSE.

DEVELOPING THE IDEA OF CHRISTIANITY AS A WORLD FAITH

If Christianity is in decline in the western world and if the local media images children receive are of small church congregations and a minority faith – and by no means all local impressions are like this – then to be fair to Christianity it is important to question certain unspoken assumptions that come packaged with this mental outlook. Some children may be genuinely surprised to learn that Jesus did not speak English, was not white, did not pronounce himself Jee-suss like we do, was Jewish not C of E and that the records and echoes of his life preserved in the New Testament are saturated in Old Testament (Jewish and Hebrew) language and quotations. And if the closed Methodist church in your town has been sold off to the Hindu community for use as a temple or to a local business as warehouse premises, and the parish church at Little Boreham Cum Curriculum now shares its priest with seven other rural churches and has a service only every two weeks, that is not the global picture. In countries in Africa, in the former communist bloc and elsewhere, Christianity is alive and well and advancing. We need to present this, not in an imperialist context ('so therefore Christianity *must* be right') but as part of being fair to the faith: what we see in our school catchment is a very small piece in a very big jigsaw.

This can be done by:

* emphasizing the Jewish roots of Christianity, including Jesus as a Jew;
* finding illustrations and emphases from the world dimension to balance what we know from the local – pictures of Christians in other countries and cultures, pictures from these cultures of Christ (Japanese, black African, etc.);
* looking at Christian leadership globally, through figures like Desmond Tutu, Mother Teresa, the Pope, etc.

ACTIVITY 5.7

Images of Christian leadership

This is intended for staff discussion or for auditing the use of visitors.

One aspect of Christian diversity is images of Christian leadership. In collective worship (assemblies) and RE, is it the case that the assumption is made that we must invite into our school the 'professional Christian', i.e. the vicar or minister? Yet there are many more lay Christians, some of whom are more readily available for school visits as housewives, early retired, sixth formers who used to attend our school etc.

Does our choice of visitors affirm the importance of women in Christianity? Does the list of visitors require change or extension?

ACTIVITY 5.8

Resource analysis

Examine briefly the teaching materials for Christianity available to you. Do they transmit a view of Christianity as a white, predominantly male, European faith? Roughly what percentage of your posters and pictures show Christianity in cultures other than western?

The *World Christian Encyclopaedia* (OUP, 1982) provides a wealth of statistical and historical summary information about Christianity around the world. For top juniors who like *Guinness Book of Records* type of digging it can be a valuable tool, with the teacher's help, as a background to all sorts of project work, for it shows the religious groups present in each country of the world, not just the Christian groups. Children with a passion for this sort of statistics approach can compare the religious presence in the Falkland Islands with that in Uruguay and work towards Maths ATs! It provides a description of how the figures have been arrived at, and provides a very detailed breakdown of the Christian presence in each country. It could also dispel stereotypes the teacher may have. There are, for instance, many more Quakers now in Nigeria than in the UK, the seventeenth century original home of Quakerism, and there are scores of indigenous African churches founded mainly in this century. From 1900 to the year 2000 the forecast is that Christianity will have grown in Nigeria alone from 176,000 to 69 million, while in the same period Islam will have grown from 4.2 million to 61.1 million, set against a population rise from 16 million to 135 million.

HOW TO DEAL WITH CHRISTIAN ORIGINS, ESPECIALLY THE LIFE OF JESUS

Once again, the teacher needs to define attainable targets! If we are trying to do justice to the complex nature of the gospel narratives, the difficulties in tracing the historical Jesus, the many gospels, Acts and letters that circulated and why the particular group of documents that form the 'New Testament' were selected and assembled together, the complicated interaction between the early Christian community producing documents for its own purposes and yet in some ways growing from and being moulded by these same documents, we are bound to fail. Yet to ignore these issues in our own planning is to reduce the biblical material we are obliged to deal with here into a simplistic – and to many children, incredible – summary. Older primary children do not naturally believe in angels in the sky, stars that lead us to places, people capable of walking on water and parthenogenesis (virgin birth). It would be a mistake to start the Christian story with these things taught *as history*. So as principles for our teaching we might identify two much more attainable ones:

to demonstrate continuity and change between the earliest Christian community and the Christian community of today

and

to set teaching about the life of Jesus in the context of the Christian community's understanding of him as Lord.

Oldest primary children can know and understand certain factors in early Christianity that have disappeared or have changed:

that there were no church buildings and no professional clergy;
that the first Christians expected that the world they knew would end and Jesus would return, within their lifetime;
that there was no Christmas festival for more than 300 years and Jesus' birth was not specifically commemorated;
that Christians were persecuted on many occasions during their first 300 years of growth and this shaped their outlook and writings – for instance, in their attitudes to the Roman Empire;
that the Bible of the early Christians was the Bible of the Jews, to later Christians known as the Old Testament, since the collection known as the New Testament was not in its finally approved form for nearly 400 years;
that the term 'Christian' did not arise for some 20 years after Jesus and that 'Christians' were known by other names, while being seen by outsiders as a sect within Judaism.

These things have changed, but other aspects of Christianity have remained constant:

the use of water baptism as a sign of initiation;
the celebration of Easter (and subsequent use of Sunday for worship because it was the day of resurrection);
the eating of a common meal in the belief that this was instituted and commanded by Jesus, using words he used;
giving to the poor and organizing relief for the needy in distant places;
trying to spread the 'good news', which is what 'gospel' means in Greek, to others.

Other aspects of Christianity arose in later centuries:

creeds as official statements of belief;
denominations, evidence both of rich variety and damaging schism;
Christian influence on western legal systems, architecture, the arts, etc., after Christianity was adopted as the official religion of the Roman Empire.

As older children understand that the birth stories of Jesus were told within a community of people who believed in him as Lord, who were convinced he had risen from the dead and were ready to interpret all his life as evidence of God in action, they will get less 'hung up' on those parts which seem unbelievable as literal truth and more into some beginning of understanding that these accounts are firstly religious statements about who Jesus is, not historical details about his birth.

So work with older juniors might include these objectives:

to show that there are two, different gospel accounts of Jesus' birth (Matthew 1 and 2, Luke 2) and that the other two gospels are totally silent about it;
to show that these accounts were written by and for Christian believers trying to show their belief in Jesus as God and man or God's son;
to distinguish between these accounts and later Christian legend, e.g. the story of the fourth wise man;
to distinguish between these accounts and pre-Christian elements within the UK Christmas, e.g. yule logs, winter parties, mistletoe, etc.

A four-walled classroom lends itself to murals separating these strands within the UK Christmas!

Work with infants will need different objectives:

to show that the birth of Jesus was not like modern births in hospitals with medical care, but risky, uncertain;
to show that his early surroundings were quite unlike those of a baby now – so he is not to be pictured in a cot under a mobile with a baby listening device nearby while Mary and Joseph watch TV downstairs etc.;
to show that he was thought to be a special baby, e.g. by the clever star gazers who came to see him.

For juniors, behind all this work will be background work not on Israel as a country but on the first Christians and their community, writing letters, passing on stories, teaching new converts, etc., to provide a context for the birth stories. For infants there will have to be a brief explanation about the different country and the different time, to get them away from either assuming a land flowing with cars and money or from the December (or more plausibly February) UK weather depicted on the Christmas cards they already know so well. For both infants and juniors this may be a long way from the traditional nativity play with towels, dressing gowns and sandals, watched by overcome mums dabbing their eyes at the miracle that their son has been – for a moment – turned into an angel, but it constitutes much better RE because it is much more sensitive to Christian origins and source material and does not need to be untaught as the children grow older. And it can still lead to good drama in an end of term spectacular.

Unit 6

Exploring spirituality

LOCATING THE DOMAIN OF THE SPIRITUAL

Most people – even professional religious studies experts – find spirituality hard to define. What spirituality is depends to some extent on who you are talking to.

 ACTIVITY 6.1

What does the term spirituality mean to you?

Can we speak of Christian spirituality? If so, what is it? Or, say, Buddhist spirituality? Or atheist spirituality?

Or is it better to avoid definition? Like poetry, it is easier to recognize than to define. We might have to be content to see spirituality as that area common to what is deepest in art and music and drama and poetry and religion and silence.

The Education Reform Act required headteachers and governors to ensure that the curriculum of each maintained school is 'balanced and broadly based and promotes the *spiritual*, moral, mental and physical development of pupils at the school' (ERA 1(2), italic emphasis mine).

Quite an agenda! In the case of the realm of the spiritual there are major questions to be addressed:

If spiritual itself is hard to define, what exactly is 'spiritual development'?
How can teachers promote it?
How can they see whether they have promoted it (i.e. is it assessable in some way)?

Should it be viewed as a cross-curricular theme?

The OFSTED criteria for inspection in this area have been published. If you do not already know them, you might like to try to speculate what they might be! To compare your answer to theirs, turn to Appendix III, p. 90.

In a speech to the national forum of SACREs at Birmingham on 5 December 1992, David Pascall, then Chairperson of NCC, said:

> To me, spiritual development is essentially to do with the development of inner self, with self knowledge, relationships, questioning our place in the universe, the purpose of our lives, and our ultimate destiny. As spiritual beings we are marked by our capacity for wonder, and our sensitivity to the thrill of the infinite. In the end, spiritual maturity is perhaps the discovery of direction and purpose in life.
>
> (Speech text page 7, Section 13)

These were interesting words for an industrialist to be using. He went on to quote Auden's spectre of meaninglessness in the poem *1st of September 1939* and to talk about the role of poetry, sound and art as mediums for expressing our deepest joys and fears.

> To ignore in the education of our children experiences which can not necessarily be demonstrated in physical form or described in words, would be to leave uneducated that whole dimension of humanity which we call the spiritual.
>
> (ibid., p. 8, Section 14)

He then touched on the relationship of this to RE:

> Questions about the origins of the universe – the purpose of life – the nature of proof – the uniqueness of humanity – the possibility of certainty – the meaning of truth – these are often explored in RE lessons. But how often do teachers of other subjects take time to discuss such issues with pupils, often leaving them with an exaggerated view of the infallibility of science and of the inadequacy of religion and philosophy as valid ways of viewing experience and existence?
>
> (ibid., p. 8, Section 15)

Pascall did not in these words define the domain of the spiritual. But he did map out its role in education: that it was an entitlement for all pupils; that it was part of a 'balanced' education; that the roots of art and the roots of poetry and drama and music are as vital to an appreciation of this field as the roots of religion; that it is part of a search for meaning wider than any isolated one of the subjects of the NC or RE. The NCC Discussion Paper, *Spiritual and Moral Development*, April 1993, identifies areas of spiritual development: beliefs, a sense of awe, wonder and mystery, experiencing feelings of transcendence, search for meaning and purpose, self-knowledge, relationships, creativity and feelings and emotions (p. 3). In pointing to the necessity for education for spiritual growth to permeate the whole curriculum, not just RE, Pascal and the NCC might have been writing a brief for the primary class teacher!

ACTIVITY 6.2

Educating the whole person

Marjon TV Unit produced a video for governor training, *Education for Spiritual Growth*, referred to in the Bibliography. It includes primary school footage. In the programme the presenter, Jack Priestley, says:

> We talk about developing knowledge, we talk about developing skills, but true education must concern itself with developing whole people, asking the question what will children become? What sort of people will they be? . . . and it's not until we include the word 'spirit' that we can talk about the whole person.

That particular scene was shot partly in Highgate Cemetery, perhaps a place to inspire the 'What's it all about?' type of question!

Consider how far the focus on the whole person could be applied to your work with children (a) across a year, (b) across a term, (c) across a week.

AWE AND WONDER AS EXPRESSIONS OF SPIRITUAL AWARENESS

It is often said by teachers that small children have an innate sense of awe and wonder, as if they 'feel' life and feel it whole, that somehow reduces as they move up the school and seems to be quite extinct by adolescence. If this is so, it is possible evidence for the hypothesis that people are innately spiritual or religious (not specifically any particular religion, nor necessarily possessing accompanying beliefs in God) but that perhaps these feelings disappear in the technologically self-sufficient society of the western world. Adults may need poetry to put the wonder into words, but for children the wonder can come from gazing into a microscope or telescope – 'science' – or from the remarkable capabilities of computers – 'information technology' – just as easily as from art or music or live drama at its moving best. But it is all rather vague and woolly and leaves the teacher uncertain as to whether they should be promoting this and if so, how to do it.

At adult level a theoretical framework for interpreting these feelings of awe and wonder in a clear-thinking way was provided in 1917 in what has become a classic book and is still in print in various paperback versions. *The Idea of the Holy* was written by Rudolf Otto (1869–1937). Otto was unusual in combining a knowledge of comparative religion with an interest in oriental thought, a high competence in the natural sciences and for those days an extremely wide experience of travel in different countries and cultures. His thinking led him to identify an area in human consciousness which was non-rational but very real. It included awe, self-abasement, sometimes even dread, and a sense of a presence or Presence. It was a mystery in the sense of a reality defying complete definition and Otto argued that this reality cut across culture and institutional religion. As has been the case with many writers attempting to describe areas of feeling, he had to invent a word to describe it and he called it the numinous, that feeling provoked by a numen. He 'borrowed' this terminology from association with the words omen and ominous. In Chapter XV of his book he argues that early manifestations of the numinous are found in beliefs in magic, worship of the dead, concerns about souls and spirits, animism (the belief that there is life or spirit within what are thought of as 'inanimate' objects – trees, stones, dolls, images, etc.) and fairy stories. At least some of these appear among the interests of primary school children!

For some children issues of this sort are part of a search for meaning, something the scientific and spiritual enquirers have in common.

> I do not know how I may appear to the world; but to myself I seem to have been only like a boy, playing on the seashore, and diverting myself in now and then finding another pebble or prettier shell than ordinary, while the great ocean of truth lay all undiscovered before me.

(Isaac Newton)

Children's search for meaning was investigated in the mid 1960s by Violet Madge. She wrote that

> young people will attempt to integrate whatever comes into their experience into a meaningful pattern, be it angels and magnets, sun and rockets, seeds and babies, aeroplanes and heaven, God and shops, Jesus and baby-sitters. This analogy-making propensity . . . is at the very root of creative thought.

(*Children in Search of Meaning*, SCM Press, London, 1965, p. 93)

ACTIVITY 6.3

The spiritual experience of children

Some of the children Violet Madge talked to provided glimpses of spirituality.

> A little girl lived in the sky. The sun was shining. She said 'I like the sun. I like the sun. I am going to praise to it.' You see she wanted to praise the sun because it was shining bright.

(Told by 5 year old girl, ibid., p. 36)

How very good of God!
(Spontaneous response to a bowl of opening daffodil buds by a 6 year old girl, ibid., p. 96)

 One morning in
lark song I heard a lovely
tone, The dark was
gowing the sun was coming.

(7 year old girl, ibid., p. 96)

If you are a class teacher, record over a period of a week responses of this sort (if any) by your pupils, oral or written. Do you want to encourage them? Were any triggered by a prompt or stimulus you provided? How similar is this sort of response to that a child may make in relation to a moving poem or piece of music?

 ACTIVITY 6.4

Loving lollipops

This is a practical activity developed by Kathy Raban with 6 year olds and included in *New Methods in RE Teaching*, p. 175 (see the Bibliography for this Unit).

 I told the children to get into pairs and then took one from each pair out of the room. Each child was given a word which they could easily visualise: a cat or a ball or something like that. When they returned to the room, they sat and held hands with their partner and tried to send the word across. This was done in silence. They were then told to try to guess the word their partner was trying to beam across. Some got it right. After discussion on the power of our thoughts, I followed it on with the suggestion 'Let's send loving thoughts to one another'. Some sat in a circle holding hands but others fidgeted, so sitting close was substituted for holding hands. I asked them for an image, 'What would be a loving thing to send everybody?' In the end, they agreed on a lollipop. So everybody imagined a lollipop to everybody else.

Try it.
The same book contains a guided fantasy for 8 or 9 year olds lasting approximately 40 minutes, entitled Journey to the Stars (p. 164). Fantasy is 'a tool in the search for meaning since it draws upon the imaging aspects of the self and speaks in the language of symbols. . . . It has the potential to deepen our knowledge and understanding of who we are' (p. 153).

Figure 6.1(a) a thank you tree.

  ACTIVITY 6.5

Progression in spiritual development

The NCC discussion paper referred to above accepts the notion that children will develop spiritually and goes on to say

Figure 6.1(b) parents visit an 'outdoor classroom'

Source: Cowick First School, Exeter

 Whilst not advocating a model of linear progression, the steps to spiritual development might include recognising the existence of others as independent from oneself; becoming aware of and reflecting on experience; questioning and exploring the meaning of experience; understanding and evaluating a range of possible responses and interpretations; developing personal views and insights; applying the insights gained with increasing degrees of perception to one's own life.

Do you accept the notion of progression in spiritual development? What possible evidences of this have you seen in children you work with? Do you think that in the notion of spiritual development in a person there lies also the possibility of spiritual regression? Put another way, could the spiritual development of a person at the age of 5 be superior to that they attain at 13?

ACTIVITY 6.6

Looking for the spiritual in science

How far is the delivery of Science AT1, with its reference to the variety of life, or Science AT4 in the strand on the earth's place in the universe, incomplete without providing for children an opportunity to wonder and reflect?

Look at a recent example of work you have done in science and how far it has left space for wonder or reflection. In planning your next work in this area how can you take it into account? Or does it have to be spontaneous?

The future of humanity lies in the hands of those who are strong enough to provide coming generations with reasons for living and hoping.
(Second Vatican Council of the Roman Catholic Church, 1965)

All people should cultivate roots of virtue according to their natures, their deeds and their beliefs.
(The Teaching of the Buddha, c.500BCE)

All wisdom comes from the Lord, and wisdom is with him for ever.
Who can count raindrops or the sand along the shore?
Who can count the days of eternity?
How high is the sky? How wide is the earth? How deep is the ocean? How profound is Wisdom? Can anyone find answers to these questions? . . .
There is only one who is wise, and we must stand in awe before his throne.
(Sirach 1.1–8, c.180BCE, Good News Bible)

How far do these quotations supply a brief for education as well as religion?

STILLING

Reference will be made to the use of stilling in RE visits (p. 63) and it can also be used on other occasions such as collective worship. A great deal of developmental work in this field has been done by Michael Beesley, currently curriculum manager at Poole Technical High School, when he was a diocesan advisory teacher in Salisbury, working with many first and primary schools. His book *Stilling* was published by Salisbury Diocesan Board of Education in 1990 and is available from them at Audley House, 97 Crane Street, Salisbury SP1 2QA. He notes that to work best, stilling requires regular practice just like the skills of numeracy and literacy require regular practice for other aspects of personal development and that they need to be introduced gradually. The book provides detailed help on this. The classroom environment should be welcoming and attractive, providing each child with personal space. Basic exercises for tuning in, relaxation, breathing, and returning to the everyday situation are provided (pp. 18–23).

One simple exercise is the Computer Screen (p. 20):

> Invite pupils to imagine that when they close their eyes there is a computer screen behind their eye-lids. They can choose its colour. On this screen is a trace line of the teacher's voice or a picture of the teacher if the graphics are very good! The trace line or image of every thought or distraction can be seen on the screen. Pupils also have a 'Break' key in their minds, and the aim of the exercise is to keep the screen completely clear for one, two or three minutes, by careful use of the 'Break' key.... Pupils are invited to share their experience in the de-briefing.

Michael Beesley provided the previously unpublished sample that follows, developed for and with KS2 children, and I am grateful for his permission to include it here. Children are invited to sit with eyes closed or looking at the floor so as not to be distracted. When they are settled and quiet, the exercise can begin.

Figure 6.2 'Stilling'

a   ACTIVITY 6.7

River creature

One way to become quiet and still in your body and mind is to focus your attention on peaceful and calming images in your imagination ... So, having just said that, I hope you'll involve your imagination in today's reflection exercises. This seems like a good kind of stilling exercise with which to begin this lesson. ... So, I'm going to invite you now to do a stilling exercise with guided imagery ...

You are walking by yourself in a beautiful countryside. ... It's a lovely, sunny day with a gentle breeze to keep you cool ... and you are enjoying all the beauty of the scenery. ... As you walk, you see up ahead a small stone bridge over a river. ... You walk on to the middle of the bridge, and look over into the water flowing underneath. ... As you look over, you can feel the warm sun on your back ...

The water is moving very slowly ... and it is very clear. You can see the plants in the water gently swaying as the river moves them ... and around the pillar of the bridge just below you ... you can see small fish lazily swimming in the current.

You notice a leaf floating on the surface of the water as it comes under the bridge. It is moving slowly ... and you follow its progress on its way downstream. See how it turns and glides. ... See the direction it takes ... and notice the details of the river bank which it passes on its way downstream. ... Your eyes can now see the course of the river as it makes its way across the countryside. ... Gently let your mind's eye follow it on its course ... enjoying the view on its way into the distance. ... As the river disappears into the horizon, you bring your eyes back again to the clear water just below you ... and you decide, for a few more moments, to watch the gentle movements of the plants and fish ... and the reflections of the sunlight on the surface ... (Long pause)

Then you look to one side, and there curled up in the sun in a patch of long grass, you see a small creature fast asleep ... notice the colour of its fur ... and its most attractive features. ... You see its chest gently rising and falling as it breathes ... and as you watch, you realise that your own breathing has quietened down and is gently flowing in time to the breathing of the animal. ... This makes you feel even more peaceful and relaxed ... and at peace with the world around you ...

Now you realise it's time to leave ... and very quietly, so as not to disturb the animal, you stand up and begin to walk away from the bridge to follow the path which will bring you back to this room ... (Pause). Now you are remembering the kind of room we are in ... and your place in the room. ... Notice again how it feels to be sitting in your chair ... with friends around you. ... But don't open your eyes until you are quite ready to come back fully to everything and everyone around you ...

Using visits and visitors

VISITS

It is arguable that people of any age best increase their understanding of religion by meeting religious believers and by visiting places of worship and other religious sites. These encounters are often memorable, even though experience teaches the teacher that children do not always notice or remember the things that adults hope they will notice and remember!

There are desirable guidelines for RE visits:

1   The need to achieve a balance between unstructured visits, which waste time and lack focus, and at the other extreme 'death by worksheet', in which children are so busy ticking boxes and completing the tasks, that they do not stand back and take in the total experience. In a place of worship this taking in the atmosphere may be the most necessary part of the visit, the part that a video or book or poster cannot communicate. That is why on arrival, sometimes a simple sitting and silent stilling exercise is the best way to start, provided of course that it does not follow several hours on a coach on which children have had to sit three to a seat, knees under chin!

2   The desire to avoid stereotypes – must the Christian place of worship always be the parish church? Must it always be the vicar who shows us round and not a member of the congregation? The verger's stories will differ from the vicar's. The synagogue security officer will bring a perspective quite different from the rabbi's.

3   Classroom work on faith communities needs to precede visits to buildings, for empty buildings are not the communities that inhabit them, and if the buildings are cold and unheated when not in use by their congregation in winter, children may gain false impressions that reduce the community to a museum, when it may be lively and expanding. What would we learn about the families and homes of the children in our class from visiting their empty house? Some things, certainly, but not others.

4   We need to teach and discuss certain social skills about behaviour in mosques, synagogues, churches, etc., before the visit. About what to wear and what not to wear, about chewing and general deportment, about the whole idea of showing respect to what others hold dear.

5   If, as is likely at primary level, the visit is part of work in more subject areas than RE, the RE element should not be subsumed under other work in such a way that it disappears. For instance, if a parish church visit were to consist mainly of the history of the building, the technology of its construction, the geography and geology of its materials, surveys on life spans in different centuries from the graves in the church yard, measurement of height, particular angles, drawing the bell tower, etc., the notion that this building has been brought into being and sustained by a worshipping community who try to be disciples of Jesus will have been lost entirely.

6   If a visit is walkable and local to the school it may be well worth doing again, for in common with good books and good videos, good visits are worth repeating – children and adults gain some knowledge or understanding on a second visit that they may have missed on the first. A re-visit provides an opportunity to develop issues and questions raised by the children after the first visit.

Teachers themselves might be unsure of etiquette for places of worship. A summary appears in the Appendix on p. 85, though it should be remembered that local variance does occur and a preliminary visit by staff, possibly a training day venture, is desirable if practicable.

    ACTIVITY 7.1

Test run

1   Select a local place of worship that you know little or nothing about that might make a suitable venue for a class visit.

2   Make contact with the worshippers. Notice boards often provide names, addresses or phone numbers. See if you can arrange a visit for yourself and, if they are willing, take a camera or camcorder to record some of the visit. Some of your photographs or video could become a preview for the class visit.

3   On your visit, see whether suitable literature to introduce the building or the religious group is available for you to buy and take away, and whether they can provide you with a national address for their religious organization that deals with school queries to supply further information.

4   Cast your eagle eye around the building. What safety or pupil conduct aspects need to be remembered in planning for 25 children to visit with you? Where are the toilets!

5   In preparing in detail for the visit consider the management of time. How much time will be available? What proportion do you want to give to a guided tour or talk, if offered? What to a stilling exercise for pupils to take in the atmosphere of

the building? What to a worksheet for draft completion during the visit? What for children's own questions?

VISITORS

Bringing in a visitor to an RE topic is organizationally far easier than taking a class out. The ideal is to do both, but there are times when the visitor must suffice. There is much to be said for not letting a visiting speaker speak! So often a prepared talk is not on the level of the children and they become bored. Or at last they get chance to ask their questions and the play-time bell goes and with it the visitor, just when it had all got going. Better to prepare the children carefully for the visitor so that they can interview the visitor rather than listen to a talk. This brings the visitor to their wavelength more quickly: 'Do you ever feel embarrassed wearing those funny collars?' may make the visitor feel at home quickly. A little reception committee of older juniors, if that is the class being visited, also helps to create the feeling that this is their visitor. A balance between women and men, lay and professional leadership figures in religions being studied also helps, otherwise we may be promoting stereotypes. Sometimes it can be a good way of meeting the person who will host the class visit to their place of worship the week after their visit to the class. They can then prepare the class in terms of etiquette for the visit.

Some visitors recur! The vicar, for instance, in a church-aided primary school, may be a weekly figure in assembly or may teach some RE. It is important for the RE programme to be clear about the status of such regular visits, if they occur. A weekly cuppa in the staffroom may be the vicar as chairperson of the governors getting to know the staff, or a weekly visit in assembly may be to make the vicar known to all the children. So might the occasional wander into classrooms while children are at work. It is only when the vicar is teaching from the RE syllabus or being interviewed in an RE topic that the visit constitutes RE. While that is very much a statement of the obvious it does rebut the very feeble claim by a small minority of schools that the vicar's presence on the premises once a week somehow constitutes RE, presumably by reflected holiness or saintly osmosis. But in RE the reappearance of a successful visitor, whoever it happens to be, can enhance pupil enjoyment and lead to a developing relationship with the class.

 ACTIVITY 7.2

Stereotyping

Consider the ways in which professional leaders in a particular faith group are presented in the media, e.g. the Christian clergy. Include sitcoms and fiction in your consideration. Are they presented as predominantly male? Middle aged? Pleasantly bumbling? Harmless? How far has Frank Williams' portrayal of the vicar in *Dad's Army* become the norm? What stereotypes have your class imbibed?

It is often the case that children growing up within a faith community – and those outside them – see the professional or lay leaders as active only in public, e.g. in synagogue on shabbat, or conducting a wedding the child may have been to. Children will be much less aware that leaders of faith communities have other, equally important, roles, which are less public: giving interpretations of their religious law; dealing confidentially with people in crisis; visiting the sick and dying. These roles vary from faith to faith. How far are you aware of them? How can you structure the visit by a religious leader so that some of this part of their work is brought out? 'What do vicars do all day?!' (p. 47) is one way of tackling this and it can be adapted to any faith. Can you think of other ways of exploring the role of the leader or member of a religious community that avoids a lecture from them?

Assessment in RE

After the Education Reform Act there was a lively debate in RE circles about assessment. Because of the subject's unique status as a 'basic subject' it had been exempted both from nationally prescribed attainment targets and from compulsory centralized assessment procedures. But the Act allowed for locally prescribed targets, through the agreed syllabus, and locally binding assessment procedures could be applied. The question was – should we bother? In the ensuing debate the following points seemed to be central to the outcome:

the view by some that you could not assess RE, or that it was wrong to try, because that would take you into the semi-private realm of the child's spirituality and belief;
the view that assessment in RE would be unworkable except as a crude assessment of 'knowledge about' religion, e.g. that Sikhs wear five items beginning with K;
a strong feeling against 'testing' in RE, especially in Key Stage 1;
a strong feeling among many primary teachers that they were already grossly over-burdened with assessments and assessment procedures and did not want more.

Against this it was urged:

that if RE was the only unassessed subject it would soon cease to be taken seriously by children, especially older ones, and by teachers and parents;
that teachers in RE are making comments, judgements, marking work all the time – in other words they are already assessing RE in various formal and informal ways – and a formalized assessment scheme could help improve teaching aims and objectives and provide sharper focus for teaching and learning without distorting the process;
that since legally the only way assessment schemes could arise in RE would be via local agreed syllabus revision and professional research and involvement, such schemes would be coming from within the profession and not by imposition from outside – this was seen as one advantage of 'basic subject' status not enjoyed by other subjects.

While this debate continued, various experimental schemes began in assessing RE. Some of these were at LEA level, e.g. Essex, Hampshire. Others were devised for groups of LEAs, e.g. the scheme produced by the Regional RE Centre at Westhill College, Birmingham, for LEAs mainly in the West Midlands area. FARE – Forms of Assessment in Religious Education – was produced for the LEAs of Avon, Cornwall, Devon, Dorset, Gloucestershire, Wiltshire and the States of Guernsey, who were found to have sufficiently compatible agreed syllabuses to enable a common assessment framework to be attempted. A team of researchers at Exeter University working with teachers and advisory teachers at each key stage in each LEA and in cross-LEA groups, roughly 200 teachers in all, produced materials which were trialled in classrooms across the LEAs within the scheme. The FARE final report appeared in 1992 and two-thirds of its 316 pages are taken up with specific ideas for each key stage that could be copied and used in school. The FARE findings then went to their client LEAs who used them in their agreed syllabus revision. Other LEAs outside the FARE group started to investigate FARE for themselves as a user-friendly scheme produced by teachers for teachers.

FARE explored and recommended various methods of assessment for Key Stages 1 and 2, sticking closely to its brief to develop **forms** of assessment in RE, not a single uniform model.

1 Journeys self-assessment, KS1

Sheets for self-assessment can be introduced at the beginning of the topic and the criteria for self-assessment carefully explained to the children. The suggested criteria are deliberately simple:

> I think I did this job very well
> I could have done this job better
> I didn't do this job very well

It is possible to undertake this sort of assessment at the end or at interim stages of the task. The Journeys sample which appears here (Figure 8.1) comes from an evaluation booklet given to pupils at the start and provides evidence for assessment by the teacher. Sue Gibson, a FARE teacher working on this, found difficulties in isolating the 'RE' work within the wider topic Journeys and so used prompt sentences like 'Do you remember the story about the girl going to Lourdes?'. She suggests as improvements planning a week's work with a main RE focus and using this sort of booklet during that week. Otherwise a folder record would store the RE pieces of work over a longer period with a teacher interview at the end before the child completed the booklet. Sue Gibson felt this method allows for negotiated statements and assessment of process not simply product, within a framework which was not too time consuming for the teacher (FARE Report, p. 115).

2 Christmas prioritizing exercise, KS1

This piece of assessment comes from a collection of assessment activities including photo activity, brainstorm, guided questions, concept mapping, concept charts, sequencing, prioritizing

Draw your special place ⁽⁴⁾

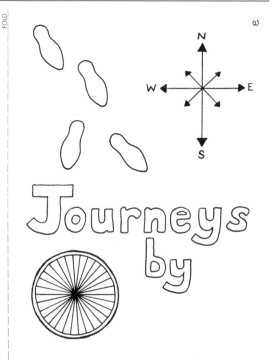

Journeys by ⁽¹⁾

Comments and Observations

Aims ⁽²⁾
- To reflect on journeys and their importance for us.
- To develop a knowledge and understanding of practices associated with worship, prayer and pilgrimage.

Specific Objectives	Teacher Comment
E1 Pupils should know that some people regularly pray or worship God in their homes or in special places. E6 Pupils should know some of the stories associated with pilgrimage.	

What I liked best ⁽³⁾

What I didn't like

What I can remember

What I want to find out about

FOLD

FOLD

Figure 8.1 Journeys self-assessment, KS1, FARE Project

Examples 11 and 12

SEQUENCING
PRIORITISING/RANKING

CHRISTMAS

The teacher writes:

"The children did not know anything about the fact that Christmas was the birth of Jesus. They related Christmas to Father Christmas and receiving presents. Our work was based on the Christmas Story and the real meaning of Christmas, including the fact that they could give family and friends presents which did not cost money, e.g. love and kisses.

I deliberately left the assessment until two weeks into the Spring Term so that Christmas had faded from their minds."

Possible teaching and learning activities have not been listed here. A developmental approach to the topic of Christmas for years 3, 4, 5 and 6 is included in chapter four.

Programmes of Study

Pupils should be given the opportunity to:

A   reflect on their own relationships with family and friends, and, if appropriate, their relationship with God/the transcendent.

C   talk about values such as love, honesty, fairness and trust which may be important in their own lives.

D   hear about, see, and listen to stories from special books of religious writings.

     hear some stories from the lives of key religious figures.

E   hear about some religious festivals, their stories and celebration.

F   explore different ways of expressing responses to events, people, and nature.

Specific Objectives

A4   Pupils should be aware of the part played by family and friends in most people's lives.

C2   Pupils should understand the importance of qualities like love, honesty, fairness and trust.

D2   Pupils should know some of the stories associated with key religious figures.

E5   Pupils should know some of the ways in which different festivals are celebrated, and the reasons for the celebration.

Sequencing

"The children were asked to sequence a series of six Christmas cards that depicted different scenes from the Nativity. Without exception they were able to put the cards in the correct order and tell the story."

Prioritising/Ranking

"The children were given a list of presents from which they could choose six for Mummy's birthday. The list included six presents that were things like being tidy and six that were more obvious presents like a box of chocolates.

By discussing their choice with them it was clear that there had been a development in their attitude to Christmas."

Note: an evaluation booklet is an alternative form of assessment which can be used within this topic. An example is included in the relevant section.

KEY STAGE 1

Figure 8.2 Christmas prioritizing exercises, KS1, FARE Project

---

THE FARE REPORT

VISIT RECORD SHEET

MY IDEAS ABOUT THE VISIT

My name is: _____

I went to: _____

I worked with: _____

I was good at _____

_____

I liked: _____

_____

I disliked: _____

_____

I think the important ideas were: _____

_____

I saw: _____

_____

I know: _____

_____

I heard: _____

_____

It surprised me that: _____

_____

I needed to know more about: _____

_____

Questions I would like to ask: _____

_____

_____

_____

KEY STAGE 2

Figure 8.3 Visit record sheet, KS2, FARE Project

THE FARE REPORT

Example 14

REFLECTIVE DIARY

FEELINGS AND EMOTIONS

Aims

To introduce the children to their own feelings about themselves, others and the world.
To help them feel relaxed and comfortable about experiencing this in a group situation without pressure.

Programmes of Study

Pupils should be given the opportunity to:

A   participate in periods of stillness and quiet thought, and, where appropriate, express their personal reflections for themselves or others.

reflect on their feelings and relationships, and be helped with this reflection if appropriate.

share their own experiences, including, if appropriate, experiences of God/the transcendent.

listen to and talk about the experiences of other people in relation to key points in human life.

B   discuss questions of meaning and purpose, especially those which arise naturally during their work or from their own experiences.

C   discuss things in life which are important to them and why these are valued.

F   continue their exploration of different ways of expressing response to events, people and nature.

Specific Objectives

A1   Pupils should be able to participate in periods of stillness and quiet thought, and explain how these may be used for reflection.

A2   Pupils should be aware of their feelings and experiences, and explain possible reasons for them.

C2   Pupils should be aware that every individual has personal values and ideals.

KEY STAGE 2

Figure 8.4 Reflective diary

This was a special year for me because.....

and artefact stimulus. It is included here because it illustrates the way in which assessment can support programmes of study and specific objectives in RE teaching.

3 Visit record sheet, KS2

This record sheet came from a topic on special buildings which included a visit to a local parish church. After preparatory work in class, the children visited the church and were shown around by the vicar. Then in small groups with adult leaders they completed a work booklet about aspects of the visit (not shown here). Finally this record sheet was completed. The FARE Report suggests that this could easily be adapted to other RE topics in KS2 and provides a list of prompt or starter phrases for use in KS2 self-assessment (p. 140f).

Another totally different method that can be used is an assessment game, recorded to try to assess knowledge and understanding in KS2. Building the Mosque, FARE Report pp. 156–161 (not shown here), is one example used during a class topic on Islam. The children work in groups on a map grid to decide where to build a mosque, taking into account relevant religious, historical and geographical constraints.

4 Reflective diary

This is included here as an example of an attempt to explore the domain of spirituality rather than just RE (see Unit 6). After a 'Let's imagine' exercise to focus the child's mind on the chosen subject, the child writes the diary entry, which should be allowed to remain private unless the child wishes to share it. These are not intended to be marked or used in teacher assessment. Other suggested prompts for reflective diaries include:

To trust others means . . .
If I had a magic wand I would like to be able . . .
If I had to tell a lie, I would only do it if . . .
When I feel happy I would like others to share my happiness by . . .

 ACTIVITY 8.1

Sequencing, thoughts sheet assessments

The two sheets here (Figures 8.5 and 8.6) are from a KS2 assessment scheme in the FARE Report (p. 168f). How might you use these with your class?

All these examples are reproduced by permission of the FARE Project.

WHAT HAPPENED WHEN?

Rearrange these statements and piece together the events of the first Easter.

Jesus was buried in a tomb by a rich follower called Joseph of Arimathea. 1.

Peter, one of the disciples claimed he had never known Jesus. 2.

Jesus was arrested in the Garden of Gethsemane. 3

A man called Simon was pulled from the crowd and made to carry Jesus' cross because he was too tired and weak. 4

Judas showed the guards which man was Jesus. 5

Peter, one of Jesus' disciples said he would never let him down. 6

Jesus and his disciples shared the Passover meal in an upstairs room. 7

Jesus shared bread and wine with his disciples and asked them in future to remember them as his body and blood. 8

Jesus rose from the dead and appeared to his disciples and friends. 9

Two women came to the garden and found that the tomb was empty. 10

The crowd called for Jesus to be crucified and Pontius Pilate washed his hands, sending Jesus to his death. 11

A Roman soldier said 'Truly this was the Son of God'. 12

Jesus was crucified with two criminals. 13

The disciples fell asleep leaving Jesus alone. 14

Figure 8.5 KS2 assessment scheme from the FARE Report: What Happened When?

Figure 8.6 KS2 assessment scheme from the FARE Report: Good Friday Thoughts

a   ACTIVITY 8.2

Assessing assessing in RE

Select an area of work – a topic or part of a topic – in your RE teaching and adapt
one of the FARE assessment exercises to it. Carry it out but then evaluate the results:

Did it help to focus pupil learning and self-assessment?
Did it help to focus how you taught the topic?
How long did the assessment part take?
How would you compare it in value with your assessment work in history or art?
What disadvantages did you find?
Could you adapt it further or produce a different form of assessment that would
have been better?

Important issues associated with RE

CHILDREN WITHDRAWN FROM RE

Most commonly the parental legal right of withdrawal is exercised by Jehovah's Witnesses, though this is not universal among Witness families. It may be that apart from the name, all that most teachers know about Jehovah's Witnesses is their refusal of blood transfusions and of the celebration of birthdays and Christmas. Appendix II provides more background information on this religious group.

Other religious groups are less systematic in their withdrawal of children from RE. Occasionally Muslim parents who think that RE in their local school is about Christian mission may withdraw their children from it. Fundamentalist or conservative Christian parents may withdraw their children from RE because they object to world faith teaching – though often when this happens it is because they think that the aim is the pic'n'mix approach described earlier, or that all faiths are being taught as 'equally true'. I have also had rare experiences of what can only be described as evangelically atheist parents who have not wanted their child to come into any contact with so contaminating, world-damaging and obsolete a force as religion (their words of description, not mine!) because they have seen RE as promoting religion simply by mentioning it.

Because some of the reasons for withdrawal stem from a misunderstanding about what RE is, it is essential to liaise with any parents contemplating withdrawal to make sure they understand what they are taking their child out of. Many JWs assume they are protecting their child from indoctrination into mainstream Christianity, which they view as fallen from truth and hostile to them and their beliefs. Some members of religions other than Christian will assume that 100 per cent of UK RE is Christian in content and missionary in intention. They will not know that this is not the nature or function of RE unless teachers tell them. Attention might need to be given to this in revising the school policy statement on RE.

ACTIVITY 9.1

Find out how many children are withdrawn from RE in the school best known to you. What are the reasons for this (if known)? What information were the parents given before this decision was reached? What provision if any does the school make for the children? (It does not legally *have* to make any educational provision.) How often is the school subjecting these arrangements to review and contacting the parents again?

RE AND COLLECTIVE WORSHIP ('ASSEMBLIES')

Schools have always assembled youngsters together for different purposes: 'praise and blame' sessions, pep talks and tellings off, celebrations, visitors, special events – all the business of the school community. These different gatherings are properly called assemblies and can occur as often and for whatever length the school chooses. But the 1988 ERA requires a daily assembly for collective worship, whether whole school, or part of a school or a class act of collective worship and at whatever time of day the school chooses. Taking a term as a whole this act of collective worship must be of a broadly Christian nature, but by calling it collective worship and not corporate worship, the Act appears to be trying to distinguish the worship of a religious community of believers, a corpus or body who have chosen to be present, and the worship of a more mixed group collected together, who have not chosen to be present. Collective worship deserves a book in its own right; our concern here is simply with its relationship to RE, if any.

A minority of headteachers – fortunately a tiny minority – tried to claim that RE could be done through collective worship. Clearly this view is highly unsatisfactory for a number of reasons. Whatever 'worship' is, it is not the same as education, which is about enquiry and discovery and the opportunity to question. Nor could one consider dealing with other areas of the curriculum solely through a mass session in assembly – Technology, for instance? Nor would an assembly for RE meet the law on worship, any more than an assembly for Geography or Science would. And since 'assembly time' in some schools is the only non-teaching time for some staff, who are therefore allowed and encouraged to be absent from it, it degrades any area of the curriculum to be delivered in the class teacher's absence and uninvolvement in the process.

Of course, sometimes class presentations or material from RE lessons may be used in collective worship, as may material from English or Drama or any other 'subject' at all. But the best schools will consider and plan collective worship and RE as separate issues even if there is sometimes overlap, e.g. at Christmas.

ACTIVITY 9.2

Are collective worship and RE clearly distinguished in the primary school you know best? Make a note of the themes taken in collective worship in a school known to you over several weeks. How far do they fit subject 'boxes'? How far are they educational? Is there any overlap with topics in RE, or complete discontinuity?

PARENTAL CONCERNS ABOUT RE

Parents can be concerned about RE and may choose to express their concerns without any real desire to go as far as to withdraw their children from the subject. They may object to teachers who use RE to put their own views across very strongly, whether these views be religious or anti-religious. They may, of course, as in other areas, get 'the wrong end of the stick' by virtue of a comment or story the child brings home. Parents who are strongly committed to a faith might balk at the study of another faith by their child, or more likely at a visit to a place of worship of that faith.

I do not wish my child to visit those people.

a parent wrote to me. The religions of the parents and those being visited could be almost any. Perhaps there was some deep fear that in one hour 'those people' would contaminate or unsettle the child. Strange that in an education system in which it could be cynically remarked that secular indoctrination goes on unquestioned for 95 per cent of the time, parents get so worried about religious indoctrination in the 5 per cent or the 5 per cent of 5 per cent which is spent on RE visits. But we still have to recognize the sincerity of these worries and attempt to deal with them. Another issue of concern among some evangelical Christian parents is the question of the Satanic and the possible evoking of interest in it in school among children that might lead out of school to experimentation with ouija boards etc. Some parents feel that jokes and light-hearted treatment of this area in school ignore the dangers of dabbling in the world of spirits. For these reasons some syllabuses or schools have banned the teaching or 'celebration' of Hallowe'en. Perhaps the issue of ghosts or spirits is irrepressible and is just as likely to arise in class library fiction books as in RE itself. It must be emphasized that by no means all Christians would oppose any mention of the subject, provided it were done sensitively, and while some would see the 'celebration' of Hallowe'en as harmless fun, it is potentially a controversial issue other parents might raise as undesirable.

 ACTIVITY 9.3

Dear Class Teacher,

I am the parent of . . . in Class 5, and I am writing to express a concern about the inner city visit proposed for this class.

I see from the parental consent slip that I am asked to consent to my child being taken into a Hindu temple as part of the RE.

I am unhappy to see the school seeming to promote a faith that worships idols in clear contradiction to Bible teaching and I am also concerned about an approach to RE that seems to place all religions on the same level as equally true. Our British faith seems to be sidelined every time. I wonder if a visit to a Moonie cult group is next on the list?

I could simply return the reply slip without my consent but as I do not wish my child to miss the rest of the visit or to be singled out as odd or different because I have raised this issue, I should prefer to see the school re-consider the trip and perhaps eliminate the temple call from it or replace it with a stop at the cathedral?

I look forward to hearing from you.

Yours sincerely,

A.N.R.Ticulate
(Parent)

You are the class teacher of Class 5. In discussion with the headteacher, how would you go about answering this letter?

RE IN THE CHURCH-AIDED OR OTHER RELIGION VOLUNTARY SCHOOL

Voluntary-aided schools have a different legal framework in which to operate, as we have seen. The same is true of independent schoools and therefore in our context 'prep' schools. They are more under the control of their founding body and the requirement that RE should be taught in accordance with the provisions of the Trust Deed means that a church-aided school will probably be following a diocesan syllabus in RE. Parents may request teaching in accordance with the agreed syllabus if there is no other convenient school the child can attend at which it is offered. As part of the diocesan syllabus it may be that more attention is given in the teaching to the origins and beliefs of the providing body of the school. A school with ready access to a church community should be using that to good educational ends in RE. Recent thinking, while emphasizing the importance and centrality of Christianity in the RE syllabus for church-aided schools, stresses also the importance of teaching about other faiths. A recent Anglican report stressed that 'Lasting harmony between the faith communities depends on individuals having a clear understanding of their own faith and a respect for the faith of their neighbours.'

Aided schools are permitted to advertise for and appoint practising members of the faith community to which they are attached. Teachers applying for posts in schools such as these may legitimately be asked to provide a supporting reference from a vicar or priest or minister or may at least be asked to be in general sympathy with the aims of the providing body. Questions about this may be asked at interview. If the current VA arrangement is extended to Islam – there are already some Jewish aided schools – we shall see provision of this nature replicated there, and presumably extended into the Sikh and Hindu communities if they feel a need for such arrangements.

Clearly for teachers these separated schools are potentially controversial. Whether they encourage the ghetto mentality within a faith and within the children attending, or whether they are based on and seek to teach a different set of values to those secular liberal humanist values that seem to form the lowest common denominator in many maintained schools, is a matter for debate. For some these schools provide an alternative to what they see as the increasingly utilitarian and materialist view of schools developing in the UK; others may see them as a divisive anachronism in a secular and plural society. Many religiously founded schools up to now have encouraged an intake wider than their foundation deed, both in pupils and staff, in some cases strikingly so. There are some Church of England aided schools in inner cities with a majority of pupils drawn from faiths other than Christianity and where the ideal of serving the community has been put above the desire to proselytize. Whether only an institution as broad and wide as the Church of England could work in this way is open to debate!

But for teachers attending for job interview in schools such as these it might be helpful to know what RE syllabus is in use, and broadly what it covers for the children you may be teaching if you were appointed. Interviewees may also glean how far denominational teaching or teaching from a particular religious standpoint is being given and to consider how far they feel able to go along with this.

Despite its name, a church voluntary controlled school is not controlled by the church but by the LEA. Trust Deed appointees to the governing body are a minority and staff are employed not by the governors but by the LEA. RE is taught according to the agreed syllabus, although RE in accordance with the Trust Deed may be provided if parents request it for their children. In theory this could lead to chaos, with some children in the class being taught from the agreed syllabus and some from the diocesan syllabus. But many church schools in practice keep and use both syllabuses, and it is known for the same church people involved in planning the diocesan syllabus to be involved on the Church of England or other denominations panel on the agreed syllabus. Anglican controlled and aided schools together comprise 4903 out of the 21,000 primary schools (DFE Survey, 1991).

Appendix I Etiquette in places of worship

Unit 7 discussed visits. This appendix summarizes appropriate behaviour and dress for various places of worship, but there will always be local variance and individual hosts or guides will differ in their expectations. It is always better for guests to err on the over-scrupulous side because hosts respond warmly to any attempt to show respect. Places which require the removal of shoes often provide storage racks or even a cloakroom ticket system. This is also the cue for the point at which to remove shoes. It is not as children expect, in the street outside!

Mandirs (Hinduism)

Remove shoes before entering the shrine area. They may be worn in other parts of the building. If offered prashad – it may take the form of crystal sugar, almonds sweets, apples, coconuts or other snack food – pupils should be encouraged to accept it with thanks (it can be eaten on the spot) and warned not to be loud if they wish to reject it. Prashad is not sacred or communion food and committed members of other faiths would not be compromising their principles by eating it. It is more like the cup of tea and a biscuit welcome in many secular homes.

Synagogues (Judaism)

Boys and men cover heads with appropriate covering – cap, hat, 'bob' cap; disposable paper skull caps are sometimes available in some synagogues for boys who do not possess or have forgotten head covering. In Orthodox (the more traditional) synagogues married women cover their heads too, so married women teachers may need to be prepared with a cap, hat or scarf.

Many modern Jews believe that the best antidote to anti-semitism is education because through visits they are making themselves better understood, so visitors are warmly welcomed. For these sensitive reasons good preparation of youngsters is especially helpful.

Churches, chapels and meeting houses (Christianity)

Men and boys should remove caps or hats. In Orthodox churches represented in the UK – Greek, Russian, Serbian, etc. – women must dress 'modestly'. Bare shoulders, low cut dresses, minis, shorts are discouraged and men too are not always acceptable in shorts. In many churches the altar and immediate surrounding area is viewed as special and sometimes railed off. It should not be entered. In Orthodox churches the altar is situated deliberately behind a screen with closed doors known as the Royal Doors. Children who treat all school outings as theme park visits will therefore need to be discouraged from going under the rail or through the doors, behind the altar, pulling open the tabernacle (wall safe containing consecrated bread), playing the organ, running round, blowing 'blatty' bubble gum, etc.

Mosques (Islam)

Both sexes remove shoes on entering. Girls and women must dress modestly: long skirts or dresses or loose-fitting trousers or jeans (but not body-hugging) are preferred; shoulders must be covered.

Gurdwaras (Sikhism)

In the ante-room to the room containing the Guru Granth Sahib (holy book) children and adults should remove their shoes, wash their hands and cover their heads – scarves are acceptable and are often available on loan. All this is done before entering the room where the Guru Granth Sahib is. Sometimes visitors are asked to make a small bow – not the full prostration made by Sikhs themselves – to the holy book on entering his presence (as Sikhs say in preference to 'its') as a sign of respect. For committed members of other faiths for whom this might pose problems of conscience – and some parents understandably worry about this – it is important to note that Sikhs do not worship their holy book, nor do they expect their visitors to do so. But they do believe that God speaks through it ('him') and thus accord it great respect. They see it as more worthy of respect than a human emperor, who might expect full prostration etc. Visitors are not asked to share that belief about the book but they are asked to show respect just as Muslims expect a copy of the Quran to be treated respectfully, Jews a copy of the Torah or Christians the pulpit Bible or the altar and immediate area. If visitors to a gurdwara are offered kara prashad, a semi-solid cold food made from butter, semolina, sugar and milk, or a cup of tea which may have been boiled with the milk – and this offer is not automatic – it is tactful to accept with thanks even if the sweetness and texture are initally off-putting to those unfamiliar with either. Kara prashad can be reserved for later consumption. Sadly a number of gurdwaras have stopped offering these simply because of loud or rude comments by visiting children. Again, like Hindu prashad, it is not a sacred food, but a sign of hospitality and welcome (some gurdwaras give sweets instead), and can be accepted by people of other faiths or none without compromising their integrity.

In all these places it would be considered disrespectful to chew or to run or wander round or touch things without invitation (pupils may unintentionally enter prohibited or sacred areas and cause distress) and often in places where sitting on the carpeted floor is the norm, it is viewed as disrespectful to sit with one's legs open facing the focal point of the room – statue of the god, holy book, Qibla wall or whatever. Loud talking by teachers or pupils is frowned on in places of worship where people may be coming in and out for private or individual prayer.

All this looks rather formidable. But experience shows that guests who are punctilious about showing respect are very much welcomed, are often shown and told more, and are pressed to visit again. In that case PSE and multi-cultural education, as well as RE, have been well served. It is also a striking reminder that the *Spitting Image* culture of the twentieth century west in which it seems that 'nothing is sacred' is not universal.

Appendix II Jehovah's Witnesses

Jehovah's Witnesses is the best known name of a movement that arose in Pittsburgh, USA, in the 1870s under Charles Tazé Russell, a haberdasher by occupation. He came to believe that the Second Coming of Jesus and the end of the world we know was imminent. These are both doctrines that are 'officially' believed in the historic mainstream Christian statements of belief or Creeds, but the Creeds do not attempt to predict dates. Russell and his associates believed that the Bible is the revealed teaching of Jehovah–God. Jehovah was his adopted way of putting vowels into the Jewish and Old Testament sacred, unpronounced name of God, written YHWH in Hebrew. By studying some of the more esoteric passages in the books of Ezekiel, Daniel, Revelation and others, Witnesses came to the view that the dates for these events – Jesus' Coming again and the End – could be calculated. Various attempts were made and when war broke out in 1914 many Witnesses believed this was the start of Armageddon, the battle that the book of Revelation says foreshadows the End. This, the bloodiest battle of all time, will lead in the end to a planet inhabited by people of goodwill, ruled over by an elite 144,000 Witnesses from Heaven. Several re-calculations of the date of Armageddon have since been necessary.

Their interpretation of the Bible is what leads Witnesses to appear in twos on our doorsteps – Jesus sent his disciples out in pairs – to provide warning and prophecy and to sell *Watchtower*, the magazine of the movement. *Watchtower* takes its name from the Old Testament Book of Habakkuk, who was called to watch world affairs. He saw in them God's hand (1.15–11) from a watchtower (2.1). Witnesses also hold no allegiance to any earthly state, and hence are conscientious objectors and as such suffered persecution, notably in Nazi Germany. Neither do they vote, as this is seen as empowering earthly kingdoms and thereby the Devil, whose power is bound up in them. Birthdays and Christmas are not celebrated on the grounds that the Bible does not command them, though presents can be and are given as signs of friendship at any time. Christmas is seen as thoroughly pagan in terms of its history and activities – holly, ivy, trees, over-indulgence, etc. Again one has to recognize the non-

Christian origin of much that has become part of the UK Christmas and the historic fact that mainstream Christianity did not celebrate or mark Christmas for 300 years after Jesus.

The famous refusal of blood transfusions is also drawn from a biblical prohibition of consuming the blood of an animal (or person), for in ancient times the blood of an animal or person was seen as its life, which explains the odd remark about Abel's blood shrieking in Genesis 4.10. In animal sacrifice it was not the killing of the animal or the burning of the inedible parts of the carcass that mattered, but the pouring out of the blood offering. So Witnesses understand blood transfusions to be a mingling of two very natures and people, rather like a brain transplant would seem to many other people. At the same time this issue seems to be under discussion within the movement.

Witnesses reject as dead, or even devil inspired, mainstream Christianity, since the mainstream has not emphasized what Witnesses see as these basic biblical truths. Hence Witnesses will appear on the doorsteps of vicars and priests to try to convert them too. In that sense they are technically 'exclusivists' (= we only are right) and do not co-operate with other churches in Christians Together and similar movements.

It is therefore not surprising that Witnesses often wish to reserve to themselves all teaching about Christianity to their children. To liberal school teachers this will always be a disappointment, for it is a characteristic liberal view that we can all, teacher and pupils alike, learn from others without compromising our integrity and identity. This principle undergirds our understanding of multi-cultural education in all its forms. So there is a major collision of values here. Having said that, when teachers take the trouble to inform JW parents about what they are doing and why, withdrawal of children is not automatic. When I explained that in one year I was going to 'do' Christmas in three large murals (pre-Christian traditions, Christian legends, and what the Bible says about Jesus' birth), the JW parents were very happy for their children to take part because I was emphasizing the same sort of very mixed origins to Christmas that has led them to reject it. But at Easter their children were withdrawn again, because of the Witness doctrine that Jesus was not crucified on a cross, as I was teaching, but on a stake.

Appendix III   Answers to questions in the text

Answers to the legal quiz in Unit 1, p. 1.

1   True, although for years the teaching profession had called the subject religious education, it was still 'instruction' by law until 1988. Perhaps replacing instruction by education, which implies open-endedness, invalidates the need for a withdrawal clause now?

2   Correct. Parents may withdraw their child. Children may not withdraw themselves!

3   True. RE after 1988 remained as the only locally determined subject.

4   False. DES Circular Letter 3/89 setting out the detailed arrangements stated that a local syllabus conference could establish attainment targets, programmes of study and assessment arrangements. These would be as legally binding as national ones, but locally derived and administered.

5   False. The Act continued the 1944 prohibition of denominational, i.e. sectarian, teaching in county schools, but pointed out that that is not the same as teaching children about denominational differences as part of their understanding of the history and diversity of Christianity. In other words you might do some work with top juniors on the origins of Methodism and how it differed from its parent Anglicanism but you could not in a county school teach from any sectarian point of view in order to propagate that view to the children.

6   True. After 1944 such councils were optional. From 1988 they were compulsory.

7   False. A teacher could serve on any of the four panels within the SACRE: LEA, Teachers, Church of England, or Other Denominations (this one includes other faiths). Some SACREs have a high proportion of teachers in their total membership.

8   True. This would mean that pupils could not be legally withdrawn by teachers to do something else, e.g. extra reading during the RE lesson or topic.

9   True. Many dioceses have their own syllabuses for use in church-aided schools.

10   False. The Act does not prescribe how RE shall be organized and taught within a school, but Circular 3/89 points out that the way in which RE is organized and taught must reflect the duty to teach the agreed syllabus and also points out that this should cause no problems where RE is taught as a separate subject or module, but that particular care will be needed where RE is being taught in an integrated form along with other subjects.

How did you score? There are not ten levels in these results!

My emphases in re-telling the Ashanti tribal story about Onyankopon on p. 32

There is a danger of turning this into a western secular or moral tale about the need to use one's intelligence properly or to preach that overconfidence leads to disaster. But the tribal tradition – which I tried to retain in my re-telling of the story in the text – retains this as a story about the inaccessibility of God. 'Why can't we see God, mummy?' or 'Where is God?' would be the likely re-telling contexts for the story within tribal life.

It could be interesting to compare it with the ancient Hebrew story of the Tower of Babylon (or Babel) in Genesis 11.1–9. This story too is about God: God's remoteness, God's disdain for humankind's pride. But there are other more concealed themes here: the origin of the strange wedding cake tiered towers or ziggurats, which were in abandoned ruin even by Bible times, the origin of different languages, and the very murky origins of the Hebrews' old enemy, the nation Babylon. Not to mention the word babble entering the English language via this narrative!

Teacher's options on the question 'How can God have a son?' from p. 40

1   Get on with your work!
     (Teacher scores zero!)
2   What do you think?
     (Good move, but they've already chewed it over, so you may hear the same arguments again.)
3   Well, on the one hand, Christians think that Jesus was the most special person ever to have lived, that he was God and man, so close to God as to be worthy to be called Son ... and on the other hand Muslims think that Allah doesn't have and doesn't need children, but they respect the man Jesus, Isa as he's called in the Quran, as a chosen spokesman of Allah, one of the prophets ...
     (This keeps you neutral, but to some extent re-states the question?)
4   Personally I think that ... but you must remember that's only my point of view. Someone else might argue the opposite way because. . . . In the end, you've got to decide what you think for yourself.

Most importantly, teachers should choose any response that makes clear that there are major differences between faiths that cannot slickly be resolved, but that the questions do matter! Far from avoiding the issue, this faces up to the questions in an honest way that does not trivialize religion by oversimplifying it. The danger is always that if religion is oversimplified in the primary school, it becomes unbelievable in the secondary school.

From p. 44, Unit 5, the diversity of Christianity

All the groups listed are Christian denominations represented in the UK. Moravians (arrived in 1737) number 3212 adult members, the Countess' group (1777) 877, Christadelphians (1848) 14,000 and Wesleyan Reform (founded 1849) 5100. These membership totals do not include casual attenders or regular attenders not in formal membership of the church. For instance, the Countess of Huntingdon's Connexion lists 25 churches with 1250 worshippers (as opposed to 877 members) and 15 ministers. These small Christian groups may be unimportant for primary RE unless one happens to be near your school, but are very important as a reminder that in the UK there are 530 Christian denominations and the number is growing. How many other denominations can you name?

Source: *The World Christian Encyclopaedia*, 1982, OUP, which also provides detailed information about how it derives its numbers, and the *Free Church Chronicle*, Vol. XLVI, No. 6, for summer 1993.

From p. 54, Unit 6, OFSTED inspection of schools' provision for spiritual and moral development

Pupils' response to this provision will be gathered through discussions with staff and the chairperson of governors, and observation to indicate whether the school

has an agreed approach to the ways in which spiritual and moral issues should be addressed throughout the school; promotes an ethos which values imagination, inspiration, contemplation, and a clear understanding of right and wrong; offers opportunities in the curriculum for reflective and aesthetic experience and the discussion of questions about meaning and purpose; makes adequate provision of Religious Education and collective worship.

(NCC document, p. 9)

Appendix IV   How SACREs are organized

The SACRE has four panels: LEA, Teachers, the Church of England (except in Wales) and Other Denominations (including other faiths). Each group has one vote, collectively. GM schools can be represented collectively but do not constitute a separate voting panel. The advice offered by a SACRE carries no statutory force, but a SACRE does possess the significant power to require a review of the agreed syllabus. Even if the LEA panel does not agree, the other three panels may require it to undertake a revision of the agreed syllabus. It is expected in addition that LEAs will work with their SACREs to review the existing provision and support for RE in their schools and some LEAs have given their SACRE a role in their complaints machinery. Each SACRE is required to produce an annual report outlining its advice and activities and many LEAs send these to every school. The National Curriculum Council provides an annual summary of SACRE reports nationwide and SACREs themselves hold an annual conference. In its early days the National Curriculum Council under its first chairperson, Duncan Graham, did not concern itself with RE or SACREs. But the appointment of a full time NC Officer for RE eventually followed and David Pascall, the second chairperson of the NCC, emphasized repeatedly his commitment to the importance not only of RE but of the delivery of the spirituality clauses in the 1988 Act. SCAA has continued this tradition of involvement e.g. in producing national Model Syllabuses (1984). See p. 95.

Bibliography

Excellent value for any primary school is membership of PCfRE, the Professional Council for Religious Education. This entitles the school to the termly magazine *RE Today*, written by and for serving teachers and including Look! Hear!, reviews of all the latest materials for classroom use in RE, also a wall poster and often a cover that can be cut out and turned into a second poster. A Worship File also includes ideas for collective worship ('assemblies'). With this can come a Primary Mailing of further classroom-related materials. All this is also available without PCfRE membership. For details of the various subscription packages and current rates contact:

PCfRE (Membership & Subscriptions), Royal Buildings, Victoria Street, Derby DE1 1GW

RE Centres

RE Centres provide updated collections of useful artefacts and resources and an opportunity for teachers to browse through them. If you are not near one, a training day excursion, booked in with them in advance, can be well spent. The main ones are located below, but there are other collections as well, some of them diocesan, that can also help.

London

The National Society for RE, Development Centre, 23 Kensington Square, London W8 5HN

BFSS RE Centre, West London Institute of Higher Education, Lancaster House, Borough Road, Isleworth, London TW7 5DU

Birmingham

Regional RE Centre, Westhill College, Selly Oak, Birmingham B29 6LL

York

The York RE Centre, University College of Ripon & York, York Campus, Lord Mayor's Walk, York YO3 7EX

Manchester

Sacred Trinity Centre, Chapel Street, Salford, Gtr Manchester, M3 7AJ

Wales

Welsh National Centre for RE, School of Education, UCNW, Deiniol Road, Bangor, Gwynedd, LL57 2UW

UNIT 1

The law

John M. Hull: *The Act Unpacked – the meaning of the 1988 Education Reform Act for RE,* from CEM at the PCfRE address above, 1 85100 060 7.
    Also DFE Circulars 3/89 and 1/84 give guidance on interpretation.

Assessment

Assessing, Recording and Reporting RE: A handbook for teachers, 1991, 0 9502706 6 0 from Regional RE Centre, Westhill College, Selly Oak, Birmingham B29 6LL.

The Main Report of the FARE Project, 1991, 0 9518041 0 3, from FARE, University of Exeter School of Education, St Luke's, Heavitree Road, Exeter EX1 2LU.

The National Curriculum and its assessment, 1993, Ron Dearing, School Curriculum and Assessment Authority, 1 85838 030 8.

For a recent RE **agreed syllabus** in line with ERA:

Religious Education: Promoting quality, published by the Education Department, Devon County Council, County Hall, Topsham Road, Exeter EX2 4QG, 1 85522 177 2.

REaction, REflection, REsponse, referred to in the text, is the 1992 agreed syllabus for Dorset, available from Dorset County Council, Education Department, County Hall, Dorchester, Dorset, DT1 1XJ, 085 2165811.

The NCC published *An Analysis of Agreed Syllabuses for RE,* 1993, 1 85838 011 1 which became controversial because of its claim that a whole crop of post 1988 syllabuses did not meet the requirements of DFE Letter 3/91.

The School Curriculum and Assessment Authority produced in 1994 Model Syllabuses for RE, first as six consultation documents: Introduction, Model 1, Model 2, Working Party Reports, Model Attainment Targets and a Glossary of Terms (not terms in education-speak but in world religions). Copies (no ISBN) from SCAA, Newcombe House, 45 Notting Hill Gate, London W11 3JB.

For RE in general see G. Read, *et al. How Do I Teach RE?,* 2nd edition 1992, Stanley Thornes, Cheltenham, 0 7487 1470 7.

UNIT 2

Starting out with the National Curriculum, 1992, NCC, Albion Wharf, 25 Skeldergate, York YO1 2XL, 1 872676 98 7.

Religious Education: A local curriculum framework, 1991, NCC, as above, 1 872676 59 6.

Newcastle upon Tyne Agreed Syllabus for RE, 0 902 653 76 8, quoted in the text, is available from Education Department, Civic Centre, Barras Bridge, Newcastle upon Tyne NE1 8PU.

For seven, detailed, suggested KS1 RE mini-topics and a discussion of others see Unit 4 in: *Religious Education in KS1 – A Practical Guide*, T. and G. Copley, 1993, Southgate Publishing, Crediton, Devon, 1 85741 046 7.

UNIT 3

A Gift to the Child: Religious Education in the Primary School, M. Grimmitt, J. Grove, J. Hull and L. Spencer, 1991, Simon & Schuster, Hemel Hempstead, Teacher's Source Book, 0 7501 0128 8, 14 pupils' books 07501 0129 6, and audio cassette, 0 7501 01411 5. This team working in West Midlands schools produced teaching materials on seven religious items, some crossing more than one faith: Our Lady of Lourdes; Ganesha; Nanak's song; the Call to Prayer; Angels; Jonah and Hallelujah. The 136 page teacher's book provides the sort of context and ways into the items which teachers will welcome.

Ronald Goldman's research in the mid 1960s, which exercised a strong influence over primary RE for decades, is referred to in two of the activities in this Unit. He wrote two books: *Religious Thinking from Childhood to Adolescence*, 1964, Routledge, London, and *Readiness for Religion*, 1965, Routledge, London, both now out of print. Part of his thesis was to try to apply Piagetian insights to RE and to try to prevent material unsuited to the particular conceptual development stage of children from being taught. Many of Goldman's answers are now very dated, but some of his questions are perennially appropriate to RE teaching.

On story in general (not RE specific) see Betty Rosen: *And none of it was nonsense: the power of story-telling in the primary school*, 1988, Mary Glasgow, London, 1 85234 191 2, and *Shapers and polishers: teachers as story-tellers*, 1992, Mary Glasgow, London, 1 85234 366 4. *Bob Barton: Stories in the classroom*, 1990, Routledge, London, 0 415 04156 2.

UNIT 4

For the teacher who knows little about world faiths, these books will be found helpful:

Alan Brown, John Rankin and Angela Wood: *Religions*, Longman, Harlow, 0 582 22341 5.
W. Owen Cole: *Six Religions in the 20th Century*, Hulton Educational, Cheltenham, 0 7175 1290 8.
R.C. Zaehner (Ed.): *Hutchinson Encyclopaedia of Living Faiths*, 1988, 4th edition, Century Hutchinson, London, 0 09 173576 9.

A Gift to the Child (see Unit 2 Bibliography) contains material on Ganesha (Hinduism), Nanak's song (Sikhism), the call to prayer (Islam) and angels (Judaism, Christianity and Islam). Buddhist writings, including stories that can be adapted for children, appear in *The Teaching of Buddha*, Buddhist Promoting Foundation, c/o Mitutoyo UK Ltd, Unit 1, Kingsway, Walworth Industrial Estate, Andover, Hants, SP10 5LQ (no ISBN).

The Junior RE Handbook, edited by R.Jackson and D.Starkings, 1990, Stanley Thornes, Cheltenham, 1 871402 31 X, has useful chapters on world faiths and how to teach them in the junior classroom. Jack Priestley's chapter (17) on story is also an excellent look at the use and abuse of story in our society.

For artefacts from world faiths to use in the classroom contact: Articles of Faith Ltd, Bury Business Centre, Kay Street, Bury. Tel. 061-7051878.

UNIT 5

Terence Copley: *About the Bible*, 1990, Bible Society, Swindon, 0 564 05725 8. This deals with 51 basic questions about the Bible. Who decided what went in? What was left out? Were the writers biased? How accurate were the copying techniques? Can we get back to what the writers wrote? And so on.

Jack Priestley: *Bible Stories for Classroom and Assembly* appears in two volumes, the Old Testament and the New Testament, with activities for children by Angela Horton, 1992, Religious & Moral Education Press, Norwich, 2nd edition, 0 900274 53 0 and 0 900274 54 9.

For the social and cultural context of life in Bible times, as opposed to the textual background of particular Bible passages or books, most Bible bookshops carry a range of on the shelf books with good illustrations. One that has been through several editions is J.A. Thompson's *Handbook of Life in Bible Times*, 1986, IVP, Glasgow, 0 85110 977 2.

UNIT 6

Violet Madge: *Children in Search of Meaning*, 1965, SCM Press, London, 0 334 00162 5, now out of print. Though dated, this book is a study of religious and scientific thought and enquiry arising from experience in the primary school years and has much useful insight and analysis.

Robert Coles: *The Spiritual Life of Children*, 1990, Harper Collins, London, surveys the spiritual life of children through their writing and drawings.

Marjon TV Unit at The College of St Mark & St John, Plymouth PL6 8BH, produced a video for governor training: *Educating for Spiritual Growth*, 1989. The subject is examined in four sections: how the term spiritual development may be understood, how it can be promoted across the curriculum, the implications for RE and the contribution of school worship to the area. There is an accompanying booklet for INSET or governors' use.

John Hammond *et al.*: *New Methods in RE Teaching: An Experiential Approach*, 1990, Oliver & Boyd, Edinburgh, 0 05 004303 X, contains much that can be used in developing spiritual awareness: stilling exercises, guided fantasy, empathy exercises, etc.

The NCC document referred to in the text was published in April 1993 as *Spiritual and Moral Development – A discussion paper*. Copies from The Information Team, NCC, Albion Wharf, 25 Skeldergate, York YO1 2XL.

UNIT 7

Making contacts for visits

A few LEAs, such as Hertfordshire, actually publish a directory of places of worship and contact arrangements, addresses, phone numbers, etc., for visits to the different religious groups on their patch. It is worth checking whether such a directory exists for your area. In a few cases guided urban walkabouts with visits to places of worship are arranged by professional centres. The Sacred Trinity Centre in Salford (address above) does this, and there is also the Interfaith Education Centre, Listerhills Road, Bradford BD7 1HD. In Christianity some denominations produce a year book listing membership numbers, clergy contact addresses, where churches are in particular area groupings, etc. They are too expensive to justify purchasing on a school budget but since the clergy get them free you can sometimes beg their last year's copy before they throw it away; it will not have changed that much and it may provide useful information for the teacher.

UNIT 8

See Unit 1 list.

UNIT 9

For more information about Jehovah's Witnesses as seen by themselves contact: The Watchtower Bible and Tract Society, Pennsylvania, The Ridgeway, London NW7 1RN, and as seen by a member of 14 years who left the movement see W.C. Stevenson: *Year of Doom 1975*, 1967, Hutchinson, London.

For a dispassionate view of other NRMs (New Religious Movements) whose children you might have in your class, see Shirley Harrison: *Cults*, 1990, Croom Helm, London, 0 7470 1414 0.

For a discussion on collective worship from a secondary context, but with primary school application, see T. Copley: *Worship, Worries and Winners*, 1989, National Society & Church House Publishing, London, 0 7151 4782 X. A staff training video pack, *Collective Worship* (four 15 minute programmes and accompanying handbook) produced by Southgate Publishing, Crediton, Devon EX17 2AF, 1994, includes primary collective worship on screen.

For church school issues see D.W. Lankshear: *A Shared Vision – Education in Church Schools*, 1992, National Society & Church House Publishing, London, 0 7151 4815 X. Chapter 4 is concerned with RE and the quotation in Unit 9 comes from page 49. Church schools and individuals are entitled to join the National Society. For details of subscriptions and membership benefits, which include the society's magazine *Crosscurrent*, write to the NS at Church House, Great Smith Street, London SW1P 3NZ.

Index